THE NEW RESTAURANT MANAGER

PART 2: NEXT LEVEL

GETTING FURTHER AHEAD

JOHN T. SELF, PHD
Professor Emeritus of Hospitality Management
Former Manager trainee, Assistant manager, General manager,
Vice president of operations, Restaurant owner

ISBN: 978-1-7364219-7-0

E-book ISBN 978-1-7364219-8-7

To Deb

Thank you for being the drive and the inspiration to accomplish anything.

CONTENTS

PART SIX
YOUR PROMOTION JOURNEY
—197—

INTRODUCTION

This is the second part of The New Restaurant Manager. This book, like Part 1, seeks to be a comfortable meeting with your personal mentor. This book continues to help rookie managers through the early stage of their career to avoid the mistakes that other new managers have made. Common situations, scenarios, and events are explored and advice to understand how they could affect careers. It also goes further by thinking strategically, not just getting through shifts.

This is written in a conversational writing style that is unusual for a career, self-improvement book. This will speed up the often-painful learning curve of new managers and reduce the number of questionable decisions and career moves.

This book helps beginning restaurant managers survive getting into management, which has its own rules, culture, and expectations that few new managers know anything about. When inevitable mistakes are made, some managers survive, but some do not.

Today's new restaurant managers are still making the same mistakes that I made when I was a new manager. Later, when I became a general manager, my new assistant managers made the same mistakes, and later still, when I became a university professor, these same mistakes were being made by my students after they graduated.

Traditionally, the only way new managers become experienced managers is by having exceptional managers who help and support. Mentors would help too, but most managers don't have the luxury of a mentor. This book strives to fill that gap.

By considering the most common situations and decision points, rookie managers can avoid common mistakes and accelerate their careers.

This book is the result of years of personal experience in restaurant management, teaching restaurant management, observing new managers, and gathering solid expertise from all levels of management. The mistakes that I made and the mistakes that other new restaurant managers made *can* be avoided.

PART ONE

NEW
BEGINNINGS

CHAPTER I

GETTING IT RIGHT

How to choose the company that's right for you

HOW DO YOU GO ABOUT CHOOSING THE RIGHT COMPANY?

This is a big deal since making the wrong choice means having a job, not a career, lots of stress, and getting a sick feeling after realizing that you hate this job knowing you have to go back to being a manager trainee again.

If choosing the right company just meant comparing which company offers the most money, it would be easy. Or when only one company offers you a job, you take the job. You need a job, they offered, you accepted. Done. But too often the company turns out to be the wrong fit because it doesn't meet your most basic need in a company.

BRUTAL REALITY

If you quit your job as an assistant manager or *even as a general manager*, you will start your next job as manager trainee. If you quit a couple of management jobs without at least making general manager, companies will mark you as unrealistic about the time it takes to get promoted, or worse, that you're missing some quality that prevents you from being promoted. The bottom line is that companies will be hesitant to even interview you for a management position. It is vital to do everything you can to choose the right company that is a good fit.

There's got to be a better way to choose a company that works for you.

And there is.

Before interviewing for a job, spend a few minutes asking yourself what really motivates you. What is truly driving you? What factor is the most important to you right now? The perfect job meets your individual needs just as you meet the company's needs.

Knowing your priority is critically important, yet often overlooked when job hunting.

Your "right now" priority motivation is probably one of these:

Work/Life balance   High pay   Environment
Fast promotion   Great Benefits   Prestige/reputation
Stable location/no transfers

VITAL FIRST STEP

It is vital to know what is most important to you, especially in this stage of your career. Your priority can and will change over time and circumstances (get a significant other, have a child, have sick relative) but knowing what drives you now will prevent you from going with the wrong company, leading you to getting fired or quitting because it didn't meet your primary need.

As an example, let's say you really wanted promotion opportunities, but a company offered you a job with better pay. You might be tempted to take the job, even though it didn't meet your primary need. If you did take it, you'd be satisfied for a time because of the great pay, but eventually you would get frustrated by the lack of promotion opportunities because money was NOT what was really driving you; promotion was.

YOUR PRIORITIES

Let's go over each of the priorities in more depth. By the time you finish this, you should have a better idea of which factor is most important to you.

PAY

Everyone loves high pay, but is it really that much more than another company? Be careful with this. Most companies are aware of how much their competitors' pay and usually stay pretty close to one another. But there *are* companies that pay *way* above the norm. When talking about high pay, I mean a *lot* higher pay than most, like 20% or more.

Mild warning: I know this may sound weird, but one problem with a company that pays *way* above the norm is that if you ever leave the company, reality will slap you in the face. You've gotten used to making this great money, making it very difficult to leave. Because if you leave, you'll go back to manager trainee and take a giant pay cut. This is super difficult for most since you have gotten used to the money. Typically, until you are above general manager, you'll go back to manager trainee. You're right, it would suck, big time.

WORK-LIFE BALANCE

Even if you love the restaurant business, sometimes you just don't want to work weekends, holidays, and evenings that most restaurant managers do. If work-life balance is most important, then definitely ask work-life questions in your interviews and in your research (Do managers work *every* weekend?).

If you don't find out, it won't take long for you to have a bad attitude when your friends or family are having a good time but you're working. Believe it or not, there are foodservice companies which offer real work-life balance. They have made it part of their culture and are rightfully proud of it.

REALITY CHECK

Achieving true work life balance at the beginning of your career is difficult, if not impossible. This is true for *all* managers, not just restaurant managers. All management positions require extra time. Managers or professionals in tech, energy, finance, transportation, healthcare, hotels, sales, manufacturing, and retail, all have intense pressure to perform. For ambitious managers wanting promotion, this almost always means working longer hours.

LOCATION

Often the ties of family, friends, or school are so strong that managers want or need to stay in one location without the worry of getting transferred. Some companies have the policy or culture that to be promoted, frequent transfers will happen. But other companies, especially large, mature companies, are ok with managers wanting to stay in one location. If stability in location is important to you, make sure to ask if transfers are required to get promoted and if you have some say in your location.

PROMOTION OPPORTUNITIES

Simple. Only interview with companies that are growing. If your priority is promotion, the only companies for you are the ones that are expanding. Growth companies will *greatly* increase your chances of getting promoted. Generally, there are between 3 and 11 assistant managers for every one general manager and 4 or 5 general managers for every one area manager.

So, every time a restaurant opens, one assistant gets promoted to GM and for every 4 or 5 new restaurants, one general manager gets promoted. If only 1 or 2 restaurants open per year, the likelihood of fast promotion is close to zero. A word of caution: past performance is the best indicator of future performance. If growth is happening or has happened in the recent past, then it will probably continue to happen. Don't let a company sell you on growth but can't deliver.

PRESTIGE

In every industry, there are acknowledged leaders. These are the companies that have super name brands, ones that your friends and family would be impressed if you work with them. The upside is that these companies are usually prestigious for a reason; they're the best, and by association, you would be one of the best too.

But be careful. Don't be completely blinded by prestige. Look at all the other factors too. Balance all that prestige with the realities of the other factors. Sometimes these companies pay below the norm or have slow promotions. Take a hard look, dig deep to make sure that prestige is worth possibly sacrificing other factors.

ENVIRONMENT

Companies have a range of environments ranging from militant to casual. With companies where everything is black and white, there is one way and *only* one way to do everything, their way or the highway. In these companies, there is little to no tolerance to be creative and no option to deviate from procedures. Some new managers thrive in this environment, others hate it. It is vital that you know which fits you best.

BENEFITS

Everybody loves benefits, from free parking to free daycare all the way to equity ownership, can all sweeten the job. Here is a sampling of benefits to consider:

- Minimum level - 2 weeks' vacation and some form of medical coverage, probably with a high deductible, few if any, employee benefits.

- Basic level – all the above, plus 401(k), complete health coverage (including dental and vision) with low deductible, good management training and development, very basic employee benefits

- Better level – all the above, 401(k) with employer matching, stock options, extensive management development, bonus, good employee benefits

- Exceptional – all the above, increased employer matching, plus significant bonus, company car, potential for equity ownership, sabbatical, paid childcare, fitness club membership, great employee benefits.

The reason that employee benefits is considered in management benefits is that employees with good benefits are much easier to attract and retain when they are well treated. Benefits may be the easiest to research since they can usually be found on company websites.

Unless you're desperate, stay away from any company that only offers minimum benefits.

Important for all companies: Your initial training and development

It is vital that new managers make sure that whatever company they're looking at has a good and thorough management training program. Ideally, you're looking for the best management training from a company that has a great reputation for developing managers in the industry. Always ask about the management training program. How long is it? What is in it? Management training is **vital** for your long-term success and essential as your foundation. Most management training programs last around 3 months as a general guideline. About a week on each position, then time in administration, then shadow managers to get ready for promotion to assistant manager.

NEXT STEP

Once you've figured out what is driving you, you're ready for the next step: researching which specific companies fit your priority. Believe it or not, there *are* companies that meet each factor.

RESOURCES

Finding which companies are known for each factor calls for you to do some serious research, but thanks to terrific resources available, the research is doable and worth the time.

Here are a few:

GlassDoor.com   Indeed.com

LinkedIn.com   Payscale.com

Salary.com   Company websites

BENEFITS PRIMER

A BIT MORE ABOUT STOCK OPTIONS

Stock options can be a big deal. They cost you nothing yet can potentially make you a lot of money.

What they are: Stock options are stocks owned by the company that are used as incentives to motivate and retain managers (and employees) with the company.

Stock options are usually given each year you are with the company. The number of stock options given each year is often based on the management level (for example, 100 if assistant manager, 200 if GM, etc.). The idea is that you will be more motivated if you have a stake in the company.

You can and will lose your stock options if you quit or are fired before you become vested (required length of time you must stay with the company).

If you're considering two companies, and one offers stock options and the other does not, I would give serious extra consideration to the company that offers stock options. In a strong, growing company with steadily advancing stock prices, the payoff has the potential to be huge without costing you anything.

A BIT MORE ABOUT THE 401(K)

How they work – This is the most common type of employer retirement plan. The company usually gives you the option of deducting an amount from your monthly paycheck. The company then invests this money which hopefully grows.

Some companies have a 401(k) that whatever percentage you deduct from your paycheck will be matched by that amount by the company. For example, let's say you make $48,000 annual salary or $4,000 monthly. If you deduct 2% of your salary each month, $80 would be put in each month. If the company matches your amount, the company contributes an additional $80 per month. This means that you are effectively contributing $160 per month. The matching amount (if any) can vary, depending upon the company plan.

Company matching money is FREE money. This is an extremely big deal. It multiplies what you actually put in. Definitely take advantage of this and take the maximum deduction. You will be surprised at how fast this grows.

Employee vs assistant manager

WHAT WOULD YOU DO IF YOU WERE GM?

You have a good, long-term employee who has just gotten into an argument with an assistant manager. The employee called the female assistant manager a bitch.

They both come to you with their side of the story.

Server: "She is always riding me. I've always done everything she's ever asked, but she never asks, she tells. Today, I just couldn't take it anymore. I'm sorry for calling her a bitch."

Asst. Manager: "It's simple. I'm a manager. He called me a bitch. He's gone. Fire him."

WHAT WOULD YOU DO AS GM?

A little context here. This assistant manager had the reputation of being aggressive and direct with employees, especially male employees. I had known about this but had never addressed this with her. My fault.

I didn't fire the server, but I did write him up. He was wrong and he needed to control himself. The assistant manager didn't like this at all. I said that I wanted to explain my reasoning, so we scheduled time outside the restaurant to talk in private. After a very rough start, we had a good, productive discussion. I told her that she was a really good assistant manager, but she could be even better if she used a mixture of management styles, and not limit herself to just the authoritative one that she used all the time for all employees. Really good employees deserve a more 'asking' tone, rather than a 'telling' tone. She would be more effective by using situational management styles that were dependent on the situation and the employee, rather than the 'one size fits all' rigid, stern, tough one that she had been using for all employees and all situations. In the days after the meeting, I could tell that she was trying, and the employees could also tell. I kept telling my supervisor how she had developed, and she was promoted a few months later.

CHAPTER 2

WHY DO SOME ASSISTANT MANAGERS FAIL?

PEOPLE SKILLS/INTERPERSONAL SKILLS

The restaurant industry will chew you up if you don't have people skills. One big part of people skills is respect for your employees. Believe it or not, there are managers who think that employees are just warm bodies; managers who only think with their own perspective, never their employees, and managers who are inconsistent and play favorites, rather than fair and consistent.

POOR COMMUNICATIONS

Managers who do not communicate their expectations to employees on the front end and then get frustrated and angry when their employees don't perform up to the manager's standards are doomed to fail.

NEED TO BE "NICE"

You cannot be the "nice guy" who never criticizes. Your employees will lose all respect for you, and you will fail. When you *don't* give critical feedback, your employees may *like* you, but they won't *respect* you.

LACK OF DEDICATION

Sometimes the restaurant industry is just not for everyone. My first management job after college and the army was in manufacturing. It was my first job, what did I know? It sounded OK, but when I actually started and got into it, I knew I didn't fit. Thankfully, that's when I discovered the restaurant industry and knew I belonged.

I loved the restaurant industry with its fast pace, lots of people contact, multiple skill sets required, instant gratification, fast promotion, good money, and every day different from the next, plus free food!

So, lack of dedication really means that a particular job or industry is not a good fit. If it doesn't fit, you'll know. It is impossible to have dedication to a job when you hate the job. When there *is* a good fit, dedication will be there.

I remember one restaurant company that started to only recruit4 manager trainees from business colleges, not hospitality colleges. The recruiters told them about the glories of managing multi-million-dollar operations and how fast they could be the general manager of a multi-million-dollar operation all while using their analysis and communication skills. They downplayed the unique rigors of restaurant management, like the fast pace, working weekends and evenings, plus dealing with a very diverse group of employees, and up close and personal with customers. What a surprise when they had almost 100% management turnover.

POOR LISTENING SKILLS

Sorry, what'd you say?

Some assistant managers have the impression that becoming a manager automatically gives them smarts and authority.

They think they should be constantly telling and not listening. Their title does give them a measure of authority, but not any more smarts. Assistant managers should be confident, but humble and practice active listening. This means to listen to what others are saying rather than thinking about what you're going to say next. Your employees have a wealth of information to share that can help you, but you have to listen first.

INTEGRITY

There is an incredible amount of pressure to meet budget goals. Some managers resort to cheating and covering up to attempt to hide the problems. But don't. Never be tempted to cover up a problem. It is just not worth it to get fired, ruin your reputation, and then tell your significant other why you're home early. When you cover up a problem, the problem is still there and only gets worse each month. If you truly can't figure out how to solve a problem, ask for help sooner, not later.

EXAMPLE

I heard of a GM who had a high food cost. He decided the way to stay in budget was to add to the Ending Inventory to lower his food cost. Normally, there are 2 managers doing the inventory, but since he was the GM, he told the assistant working with him to take a break when he did the meat portion of the walk-in. The first month he added one case of steaks to the Ending Inventory to make his food cost come out within budget. He didn't know that cooks were stealing steaks, so the problem remained. The next month, he had to add 2 cases to the EI, and the next month 4 cases. By this time, it was so out of hand and so obvious what he was doing that he was fired for cheating.

DIFFICULTY BUILDING OR LEADING TEAMS

Your job is to build your area into an efficient and productive team with high morale giving great customer service. You've got to get your employees to trust you, on your side, and working with you to achieve your area and restaurant goals. It's all about your employees trusting you so that you can get the results you need. Managers who cannot get their employees to trust them and work for them are sure to fail. This is covered in several chapters.

INFLEXIBLE

Are you the type who would argue with a pork loin? Do you tend to be such a perfectionist or so black and white that there is no room for gray? Do you believe that a rule is a rule, whether it feels right or not in a particular situation?

Restaurant management is going to be tough for both types. Since restaurants are all about people, there has to be some gray and there are few things that can be perfect.

LACK OF FOLLOW-THROUGH

Think about how frustrated you would be if you were GM and you had to always worry about one of your assistants not finishing what they started. You would have to take time to constantly check up on this manager. If this happened a lot, you would write this assistant manager off of ever being promoted and would question why they're still working there. If you can't be relied on to do what you're supposed to do, there is no hope. Don't be this manager.

FAILURE TO CONSISTENTLY DELIVER RESULTS

If you meet budget one month, then don't meet it the next month, then meet it the next month, something's wrong. To me, it means that you are not in control of your area and more importantly, you really don't understand why you are or are not meeting budgets.

I never worried about a manager if they knew why they were over budget because as long as they knew why, I knew they would and could fix whatever problem caused them to be over. But, when a manager did *not* know why they were over or under, I knew it was it had just been luck that they were under budget and if they were over budget, I had no confidence they could get it back. They didn't know why they were over or under.

- We had a lot of turnover last month, so labor was over budget because of so much training. We are fully staffed now, so will be good this month

- One of the employees was caught stealing steaks and it hurt food cost. After starting several new procedures, that problem is solved.

- We were short staffed for a while, so labor cost was over because I had to have employees work overtime to cover shifts. We hired 3 more and will not have any overtime this month.

CANNOT BALANCE FAMILY AND CAREER

Working holidays, weekends, and nights can be brutal on relationships. Just like the military, there are a lot of family routines that need to accommodate restaurant management schedules. Your significant other has to understand the nature of your work which can be viewed as a severe challenge or just part of the job. Either way, if it doesn't work, it doesn't work. No judging.

WANT PROMOTION TOO SOON

Some assistants have an unrealistic sense of their own readiness or an unrealistic speed of their company's growth and expansion. Either way, they are going to be angry, disappointed, and frustrated when they are not promoted as fast as they think they should.

BURN OUT

This is the only one that I don't blame the assistant; I blame the company or the GM because the assistant does not control his or her schedule. I've had GM's schedule close – opens and some never give holidays or weekends off to their assistants. I worked for a company where the policy was that new assistants only did closing shifts; never an open, for months. How incredibly pointless. These assistants never placed orders, never handled deliveries, and a million other duties that only happen during the day, not to mention working only nights is a real grind that takes its toll on the assistant's attitude and family.

I've had arguments (I mean discussions) with restaurant chain CEO's who thought that working really long hours with no weekends off was a form of initiation, a way to weed out managers who couldn't cut it or lacked dedication to the industry. I pushed back saying that attitude is exactly why the restaurant industry loses many very good, very capable managers who leave for other industries. Restaurants should not treat their managers as boot camp. You should absolutely avoid restaurant companies that have this attitude.

Take a hard look at each one. If any are giving you trouble, reach out and start working on it!

CHAPTER 3

SEPARATING YOURSELF FROM THE PACK

Every shift equals your career

You're ambitious. You're hungry. You want promotion as soon as you're ready. Of course, you do. That's great.

But guess what? It comes at a price.

That price is trying your best every shift and getting better every shift. Trust me on this. If you bust your butt every shift with a focus on the end game of promotion, you'll get there because your brother and sister managers will *not* bust their butts every shift. They might occasionally, but not every shift. And definitely not intentionally or with focus. As for volunteering to do things they don't like to do? Fuggetaboutit.

So, embrace your competitiveness and drive on.

The key here is to be focused. If you're good at something, great. Concentrate on what you're *not* good at.

Enough already. Let's get better.

FOCUS ON DOING WHAT YOU'RE *NOT* GOOD AT

Ask for assignments or projects that you suck at. Hate doing inventories? Do it every month. Hate doing budget projections? Ask to do it every month.

What?! You've GOT to be kidding me!? I hate them!

Yes, but your fellow assistants hate them too! That's a good thing because you're going to get good at something you need to get promoted while your fellow assistants avoid them. Talk about a great opportunity for you!

There *is* a little pain involved at first, but the reward of pulling away from the pack, differentiating yourself and getting promoted should help ease the pain. And as you do something you hate more and more; an incredible thing happens. You won't hate it anymore! Magic!

NO PAIN, NO GAIN!

In baseball, if you're great at hitting, but not good at fielding, which one do you practice? You practice what you're not so good at. To be a GM, you've got to be good, or at least adequate, at everything. If you really want GM, don't avoid something because you don't like it or are not good at it.

Have the attitude that this is a great opportunity to differentiate yourself. Your GM will appreciate that you ask for tough assignments, rather than hiding in the walk-in. Once your GM notices that you're sincerely trying to get better, your status just went way up. Differentiate? Check.

EVERYTHING YOU SAY AND DO IS A REFLECTION ON YOU

Think about what you say and do. Filter what you say and do by picturing your GM listening and watching what you say and do. If the GM would approve, keep saying and doing it. If you wouldn't want the GM to see you or hear what you're saying, don't say or do it.

Double check every email or text. Make sure they go out with zero typos or misspellings. Before you get into work, take another look at yourself. Looking good? Double check the clothes you're wearing, the way you look, and the way you carry yourself. These are the small points that can separate you from the other assistants.

FOLLOW THROUGH

When you have a task, get it done. All the way, from A to Z. You want the reputation that when a task is yours, it is as good as done. Your GM never worries and does not have to check on you because your GM has total confidence in you. If anything stands in your way, let your GM know asap. Follow through is super important and is a foundational trait necessary for promotion.

NEVER PROCRASTINATE

It's hard not to procrastinate on things you hate to do or find unpleasant. Just grit your teeth and do it. Stay 5 minutes longer and get it done. You'll help your reputation, and you'll have no stress when deadlines are due.

EXCUSES ARE FOR THE OTHER MANAGERS

When you make an excuse, you're saying that other assistant managers would have done the exact same thing as you did. Examples: I was late because of traffic. The customer left upset, but I did everything I could.

But another manager just might have left 30 minutes earlier. Another manager would have found some way to have the guests leave on a positive note, not just give up.

Remember: you are in control of your own situations. Excuses are for *other* managers.

IT'S NOT ABOUT YOU

During your shift, it's about your employees and your guests, not you. When you embrace the idea that your employees come first and not you, you're on your way.

GIVE RECOGNITION

This costs nothing yet is so powerful. Your employees deserve recognition for their accomplishments and in doing a consistently good job. Make your best people visible and treat them in ways that show respect.

But I'm not warm and fuzzy!

You don't have to be warm and fuzzy to be a great manager. Employees want fairness and consistency over warm and fuzzy.

Your GM is looking at each assistant with 2 questions:
Who has potential to be a GM?
Who is ready to be GM?

It is vital that you demonstrate that you have the potential to be a GM.

YOUR GOAL IS TO DIFFERENTIATE YOURSELF FROM THE OTHER ASSISTANTS

This is not just separating yourself from your fellow assistants in your restaurant, it is about separating yourself from ALL the other assistants. Here's a good start.

Start by being a preventive manager. Preventive managers have smooth shifts because they have prevented most crises from happening. Smooth shifts have the important side effect of allowing the preventive manager to accomplish more than the crisis manager: they simply have more time to do more and are doing so in a much less stressful environment.

> **WARNING:** Because your shifts are smooth, some employees won't understand *why* they are smooth and only see that you don't appear to be doing much. To combat this, get to know the key players (the employees who the GM respects and listens to) and make sure you casually talk to them during shifts about some of the things that you did to make the shift go smoothly. This will prevent them from telling the GM that you don't do much.

PART TWO

SETTLING IN

CHAPTER 4

THE AWESOME POWER OF FIRST IMPRESSIONS

Here's the reality of your first week on the job. In that small window of time, you will be categorized by the most important person currently in your professional life, your GM.

This is true for all companies, not just restaurants. It is true anywhere that has employees and bosses. Your GM will categorize you into one of three categories: promotable (potential star), not promotable (At risk of losing your job), or "the help" (keeps job, but no promotion).

This is absolutely not fair, but it *will* happen and even worse, these categories are based on the GM's first impression. That sounds like an exaggeration, but it isn't. The reason the first impression is so powerful, is that once a first impression is made, it is really (really!) tough to change. This is why the first impression is the single greatest influence on your beginning career.

It has always been difficult to build a successful and personally satisfying career, but it is especially difficult in this age of uncertainty. A major roadblock that affects many managers, is when they are surprised to find they have been categorized by their GM as not promotable or as "the help". It is daunting (and depressing) to think of building a career when the GM has a negative perception.

Here's an example:

A tale of two assistant managers.

Two assistants start at the same time with roughly the same experience and education. The only difference between them is that on the first day, one gave a good first impression, but the other was a little late, dressed a little out of sync with company culture, and gave off a casual attitude, giving the GM a negative first impression.

After a few months, both were doing fine. But one day, they both made the same error in judgement. However, the GM had totally different views of each.

The assistant manager who had made a bad first impression reinforced the GM's negative first impression, causing the manager's reputation to fall even lower. Why? Because the GM was *expecting* this manager to screw up and just proved the GM right ("I *knew* he was a screw up").

However, the manager who had made a good first impression, survived this error in judgement without damaging her reputation. The GM actually thought this mistake might be good for her and make her a better manager. Her good first impression shielded her from this one mistake.

First impressions are powerful.

SELF-FULFILLING PROPHECY

One of the worst results of being negatively labeled by your GM is that it can ignite a "self-fulfilling prophecy". Once started, this cycle is difficult to reverse. This starts when the GM picks up on something the assistant said or did; maybe an attitude, maybe a late employee schedule, possibly just a misinterpretation of a comment, but some behavior was the tipping point, making the GM think less of the manager. From then on, this manager is labeled as a low performer. The GM now *expects* low performance and consequently pays less attention, gives fewer opportunities to perform, and is more critical. Because the GM ignores the manager, the manager begins to doubt his or her own abilities and self-worth and consequently performance suffers. This decline reinforces the GM's negative perception and consequently gives the manager even less attention and is even more critical and so on.

If this self-fulfilling prophecy is allowed to continue, it can lead the manager to continue to reinforce the negative labeling to the point of no return, leading to termination or quitting.

FIRST IMPRESSIONS ARE REAL

First impressions aren't new; you've probably heard that first impressions matter all your life. The significance and the long-range implications of first impressions are real. For once categorized, it is very difficult to move out of that category, good or bad.

THE AWFUL TRUTH OF LABELING

At some point, you may realize your GM does not see you as promotable. You come in every day, often stay late, seldom complain, do your job, and get along with everyone, yet promotions don't happen. Why? The reason may be that your GM has categorized (or recategorized) you as not promotable or just one of the 'help'.

YOU KNOW WHO THEY ARE

Think about the people you work with. You probably know who the promotable ones are; the managers the GM thinks can do no wrong, the ones the GM recognizes in meetings, the managers who get the choicest assignments. You want to be that assistant.

THE CATEGORIES

Everyone seems to be able to see *other* managers in terms of being "promotable", "not promotable" or "the help", but we all have trouble categorizing ourselves.

Typically, managers are divided into the following categories:

- **Promotable:** the GM thinks this manager has potential to be promoted. The GM gives obvious individual attention and recognition, makes eye contact in meetings, and seeks feedback or opinions from this manager in public. The GM develops a personal stake in the success of these managers.

- **Hired help:** does average to good job, but for some reason, the GM does not perceive as being promotable. The GM shows little personal attention and gives little recognition. If the hired help does receive positive feedback, it is generally done as part of a group, not individually recognized. The hired help just pulls shifts.

- **Not promotable:** This manager is at risk of losing his or her job. The GM shows no interest and spends no time with this manager and is usually ignored in meetings and might even be publicly criticized.

You may be categorized as Not Promotable if you have:

- Noticed that your GM has a change in attitude towards you
- Kidding remarks that hurt

- Been passed over for promotion, yet received good evaluations
- A feeling that you are being excluded from some information that you usually get
- No eye contact by your GM in meetings
- Not invited to some meetings that you used to attend regularly
- A gut feeling that your GM does not recognize you as one of the best

KNOW WHERE YOU ARE

The first step is to know the category that you have been slotted. If it is negative, you've got to change it immediately with proactive actions to reverse the negative perception. This was covered in depth in The New Restaurant Manager, Part I. The personal power that this awareness can give you cannot be overstated because, once known, a manager's approach to their career changes from passive to active, from *no* control to *taking* control.

These actions, combined with a strategy to jolt the GM into noticing you positively, can enhance higher levels of job performance by understanding the GM, seeking out situations that can help your career, and positively persisting when faced with obstacles. Knowing your category allows the new manager to anticipate obstacles and start making positive changes.

STAYING AWARE

New managers should not be passive about their own careers. In the final analysis, it is the new manager's responsibility to manage his or her own career.

For each individual manager, this means staying aware of his or her own perception at work and, if necessary, aggressively working to change that perception in meaningful ways that benefit the company and themselves by continuing to consistently grow their skills and behaviors.

Proactive career management means knowing and using your strengths, being aware of your weaknesses, and continually improving.

NOT A VICTIM

Even with a negative perception, the one position that you absolutely cannot take is one of a victim. Being a victim means you have given up, that you believe that your situation is beyond your control. The truth is that everything is within your control. You *do* have control, you can and will have choices. It just means that you must take charge of your career. Keep reading.

FEAR OF THE UNKNOWN

When categorized as either "the help" or not promotable, the feeling of uncertainty can be powerful. It is this uncertainty that must first be addressed by getting to *"know"*. By the "know", I mean that you're not guessing. For when you "know", you can take effective actions with confidence instead of making rash decisions that may actually hurt your reputation.

It is the fear of the unknown that leads to the self-fulfilling prophecy of failure that causes great career damage.

Stealing Employee

WHAT WOULD YOU DO?

You discover one of your very best cooks, who has been a great employee for over a year, is trying to steal some steaks in her purse. I happened to see her go into the walk-in at the very end of the shift, when almost everyone was gone. With a purse. Odd.

I waited just a minute before walking in and saw her put 3 steaks into her purse.

She was stunned. I was stunned.

You know that she is a single parent and barely making ends meet.

She tells you that she really needs the job.

What would you do?

WHAT I DID

This is one of those situations that seems so black and white yet has some gray.

I was deeply disappointed that someone I had worked closely for over a year could betray me. I had trusted her, never thinking she was capable of stealing.

She was visibly upset, and I was angry that she would do this. I took it personally.

I talked with her about my loss of trust and how personally disappointed I was.

She promised this was her first time, that it was for a very special occasion, that she could not afford steaks, and she was shocked and disappointed in herself.

I tried to calm down.

I took the steaks back and told her that I would have sold her the steaks at cost if she had only asked.

I decided not to fire her but did give her a written warning that would be put in her file. I told all the other assistant managers what happened.

She still had her job but would have an uphill battle to earn back my trust. This incident also caused our relationship to change drastically, from friendly to strictly professional.

REFLECTION

I would do the same thing today, but there *is* a 'depends on' part.

If I had caught her with even one other employee present and not just me, I would have taken a much harder position. I'm not naïve enough to think that this was her first time stealing, she could have been stealing for months. I would have terminated her based upon company policy. But at least this time, I gave her the benefit of doubt. I admit that my bias was to believe her because she was a single parent, a minority, and I liked her, but not great reasons to go against company policy.

I also thought about different circumstances. What would I have done if I had caught a bartender stealing bottles of wine? Would I have been so lenient? No, probably not. I would have terminated the bartender on the spot. Situational morality, I know, but there it is.

What if it had been one of my assistants and not me, that had caught her and just gave her a written warning or had terminated her?

First, the assistant should tell me exactly what happened as soon as possible. I would have listened and gone over the points about probably not her first time stealing, good employee, single mother, caught alone or with other employees, etc. The bottom line is that we would discuss it thoroughly from all perspectives, and let it stand, whichever the assistant's decision had been.

CHAPTER 5

FOCUS AND AWARENESS

Know what you're doing and why you're doing it

A
s a new manager, it is easy to get distracted and overwhelmed. To avoid this, go into each shift like it is the most important shift you've ever worked. Big smile, confident, lots of energy, and obviously caring for your employees and your customers. The way you approach the shift affects your employees who then forwards whatever attitude they have to their customers.

SEE THE BIG PICTURE

Many managers go to work, work hard, stay late, go to work, work hard, repeat. They firmly believe this will get them promoted. When I first started in management, I thought so too. I had tunnel vision, looking straight ahead and down, able to see only one step ahead. This is no good. This is like playing chess when all you know is checkers.

While some assistant managers will get promoted occasionally by taking the slog approach, a better way is to take control of your career. This is covered in Chapter 23, Your Journey to Promotion and in the previous book. But for now, consider looking ahead to your first promotion to GM. You want this promotion to happen intentionally and planned, not by chance, and sooner, rather than later.

YOUR ROLE IS DIFFERENT NOW

It doesn't matter how you got into management, for once in management, your role changes completely.

Your success is no longer about your own personal achievement. It is about enabling others to succeed. When you can do this, you will get promoted, but this is a tough concept to grasp and even tougher to do when just starting out.

IN THE BEGINNING

I suggest at this beginning stage of your career that you focus on your promotion to general manager, rather than some vague 5-year plan. To get promoted, you've got to know what your company and your GM expects of you.

Many managers *think* they know what is expected, but they don't really *know* what is expected to get promoted. It is up to you to find out what is expected and required to get that first promotion. Be aware of what the company in general and your GM specifically is looking for in a promotable manager. Some restaurant companies have this formalized with a rough timetable, but many don't. One good thing, at least in my opinion, is that restaurant promotions are *not* given just because they have been there the longest.

BE CONSISTENT

I have seen a few really good new managers lose promotion opportunities because they allowed themselves to put their jobs on autopilot. They did an adequate job, but it was obvious that they were just getting through each day, being *re*active, not *pro*active. Don't get in a cycle of busting your butt then relaxing. Stay focused and stay sharp every day. It pays off.

You don't want to miss a promotion opportunity because you relaxed and on autopilot.

STAY FOCUSED ON YOUR AREA OF RESPONSIBILITY

Many of us tend to get distracted or spend time in other areas away from our areas of responsibility because we particularly like those other areas. Most restaurant managers by nature want to help. But hold on. Before you offer to spend time helping outside your own area, make damn sure your own area is in great shape.

Maybe you really get into programming the POS, but it is not in your core area. If helping others to program forces you to spend a lot of time away from your primary duties, you've got to say no. A better alternative might be to volunteer to give a programming workshop to the managers. This could show the GM that not only are you good in programming but that you're a team player willing to share your time and knowledge.

Keeping focused on your area prevents you from having your priorities questioned if your area is not quite excellent. Why did you spend time away from your area when your own area needed attention? You might answer that you were just trying to help, but again, your sense of priorities will be questioned.

The bottom line is that you've got to make sure that helping does not take away from your own area. It is great to be good at something and willing to help, but keep in mind that if your area is not 100% good, then your priority is to your own area. The exception, of course, is if the GM requests your help.

AWARENESS AND WEAK AREAS

Be aware of any tasks, skills, or areas that you to need to improve. If you need help to bet better, ask for help. This demonstrates a self-awareness and willingness to seek help in order to get better, which is a strength, not a weakness. Some managers try to hide their weaknesses, but the better path for promotion is to proactively improve. Your GM will notice.

- Admit when you're unfamiliar with a term or process
- Ask for coaching or training when you need it
- Share your strengths and offer to help other managers

JUST BE YOU

Everyone knows you're the new manager. It's OK. It is important for you to know that it is OK. It is especially OK for you to feel comfortable saying, "I don't know" because no one expects you to know everything (at least now).

But it *is* essential that if you don't know something, you find out ASAP. Make it a priority to find the answer and then get back to whoever asked ASAP. This is not a time to be cocky, arrogant, or condescending. Humble, but confident, is the way to begin.

TRAITS OF A PROMOTABLE MANAGER

Want to get promoted? Here are 17 points necessary to get ahead. I guarantee that your GM expects anyone who wants to be promoted to exhibit these traits. Work on incorporating each one into your daily management.

A promotable manager:

Gets better every day. Work on the fundamentals.

Is not defensive. If you are criticized for something that you did not do well, just listen, learn, and don't do it again. This is one time to just listen. In most cases, anything you say will come out wrong.

Does more than expected. Whenever possible, do it *better* than expected. If it is due Wednesday, turn it in on Tuesday. If it supposed to be written up, proof it, then proof it again. If you get known for doing things well and always better than expected, your reputation grows.

Anticipates problems. Many good managers are good at putting out fires. However, promotable managers *anticipate* the fire and prevents it from happening in the first place.

Attempts to handle problems yourself. Don't go running to your GM with every little problem just to make sure you get it right. If it is your responsibility and authority, handle it. If you're not sure about something, definitely ask for direction, but think your questions through *before* you ask.

Takes being at work seriously. It is great if you have a funny or talkative personality, but make sure your humor is appropriate and in moderation. Your GM wants you to be effective at management first, humor a distant second.

Is always punctual. This is a given. Your GM expects you to be dependable with no worry at all about whether you will be there on time. Being late because of power going out (have alarm with battery) or a flat (leave in time to fix it) just doesn't cut it. NO excuses. This is a foundational trait, with no slack.

Does not let yourself become a squeaky wheel. Don't get a reputation for complaining. No one likes complainers. Choose your battles and try to solve problems, rather than complain about problems. If you do complain, make sure you have a solution to your complaint.

Understands "GM language". When the GM says something like "I'd like you to…." That means do it and do it now.

Learns what others are doing. Keep learning. If you have any challenges in your area, find which managers do it well and contact them. This is smart management, not weak management.

Gets along with others.

Is discreet. If a fellow manager or your GM ever tells you something in confidence, honor that confidence. It is not worth the instant gratification to lose the GM's confidence. When I was GM, I would always tell trusted assistants what I had heard from higher up with the understanding that the first time I heard that it was repeated, they would never get information again. Not to mention badly hurting my confidence in them.

Does not hold a grudge. Get over it. Grudges just hold you back and not let you go forward.

Reads industry news websites and publications. How else can you know what is happening in the industry? How else can you know enough to talk intelligently with your GM or your GM's boss? Want to impress? Know which trends and problems are happening in the industry, and who the movers and shakers are in your industry.

Get to know your peers. You will be surprised what you can learn and what opportunities will present themselves.

Does not make assumptions. Don't guess. Your GM would much rather you admit that you don't know. Get out of the habit of saying, "I think it'll come tomorrow", or "I think she did it". Check to make sure.

Dress professionally. This is how you present yourself to the world. It is amazing how important this is. Don't neglect looking good, regardless of how casual the dress code may be.

Walked check

One of your servers tells you in the middle of a shift that he just had a 'walked check'. You comp the check and then later remember that this same server had another walked check a couple of weeks ago.

The next day you're talking with the other managers and all of them said that they too have had walked checks with this same server.

WHAT WOULD YOU DO?

What I did

No server has this many **legitimate** walked checks in such a short time. No one.

We realized this server was scamming us. He had been careful to make the walks with different managers in the hope that we never discussed it. He was right until he wasn't.

We decided to give him two written write-ups based upon his two latest "walks". This meant that he would not be terminated until he had a third write-up (for anything). For some reason, no more walks. Amazing.

REFLECTION

Always write up any server who has a walk, even if it is legitimate, which 98% are. The reasons to write it up is to document the walk, let servers know that you track walks, and hopefully prevent servers from using walks to make a few extra bucks. Walks usually happen when a server leaves their area for an extended period of time and often. That encourages customers who might only **think** about walking to actually walk because they're given such a golden opportunity.

But, determined, intentional customers who come in knowing they will walk, **will** walk. There is just about no way to prevent them; they're that good, but thankfully rare. The way to prevent customers who **might** walk is to have your servers to tell someone anytime they have to do something that will take them out of their station for an unusually long time; busser, manager, host, or another server, to keep an eye on their station by walking into their station and obviously looking around.. It's not perfect, but it **does** prevent most wannabe, casual walks.

CHAPTER 6

KNOW YOURSELF

What you hate, what you love

Every manager knows there are parts of their job that they like to do. These *usually* turn out to be the parts that they are good at.

And they know what they *don't* like to do which *usually* means they're *not* good at it.

We all tend to gravitate to what we're good at and avoid what we're not good at. But, because you're serious about your career, you'll fight this. When you can recognize what you tend to avoid, but can hang in there, do them, and become good at them, you will have taken a giant management (and personal) step forward.

Does programming the POS give you a headache just thinking about it? Does handling a customer complaint make you want to go check the walk-in?

If you can relate, you've probably gotten very good at avoiding what you don't like.

SUCK IT UP

But don't. Embrace the pain. In fact, seek them out as opportunities, not as hassles to be avoided. 99% of the time the reason you hate doing something is because you haven't done it enough. At worst, it will be a pain in the butt for a short while but at best, you'll learn something that you need to know. Do you usually go to a particular server or another manager for help with something? Now you won't have to. Remember the old saying: Knowledge is power. You better believe it.

Instead of avoiding tasks that you don't like, suck it up, (deep breath) and push yourself to get good at them. Surprise everyone (including yourself) by volunteering to do those tasks. Guess who will be good at something others are not good at? Yep. You.

Remember, you're trying to differentiate yourself from the other assistants. You'll get the reputation for being willing to tackle even the toughest jobs when others avoid them, but the best motivation is knowing this will significantly accelerate your career. Short term pain for long term gain.

When you really hate doing something, that's the one to grab! If you hate it, you better believe other assistants hate it too! That's great! You'll add another tool in your toolkit that puts more distance between yourself and the other assistants, and you're better equipped to be a better, all-around manager. Totally win-win.

MAKE A LIST

Make a list of essential procedures or tasks that you don't like to do or are not good at. Whatever they are, go to your GM and aggressively seek them out. I'll bet you'll be good at them much sooner than you thought, and surprise! You'll now like it. Try not to look too smug.

When I first started out in restaurant management, I tried my best to avoid dissatisfied customers. But, after a short while (and being severely chewed out by my GM), I knew I had to overcome this.

I knew I had to force myself, so I put myself in a position that I could not avoid interacting with customers by announcing to my servers, bartenders, and bussers, that if they felt that any customer was not satisfied, to come to me and I would talk with the customer personally.

After a period of serious discomfort, it didn't take long to get comfortable with this part of management. Eventually, I actually looked forward to talking with dissatisfied customers, turning a weakness into a strength.

As an FYI, as a manager, remember you have the authority and power to be able to fix just about anything. NOTE: Make sure to ask your GM what limits you have regarding what you can and can't do for dissatisfied customers.

OPPORTUNITY

It is probable that if you are not good at a particular job or procedure, other managers are also not good at it. This is an excellent opportunity to set yourself apart by getting good at something that other managers hate.

I will just about guarantee that when you force yourself out of your comfort zone to attack something that you don't like to do, you will feel great that you did it. Another benefit is that you could share this knowledge with other managers, giving you another competitive advantage.

I'd love to tell you that someday you'll start to enjoy every aspect of your job, even the ones you hate. But I won't because it's not true. But what will happen is that when you overcome your hate and do it anyway, you will be in a much better promotable position than you are today.

But to get there, you'll have to dedicate time and energy in activities that you don't really like doing. Whatever you must do, however annoying or difficult it is, if it is part of your job it matters in some way. So, do it and sooner is better.

You should feel great that you mastered a task that others won't or can't.

PERSPECTIVE

There are two ways you can look at forcing yourself to do things you don't like to do. You can complain, procrastinate, and develop an attitude. Or you can accept that it is part of your job, make the best of it, and do what you need to do. Either way, in the end, you're going to have to do it anyway, since it is part of your job. But one attitude leads to being miserable and frustrated, while the other leads to promotion. Your choice.

PROCRASTINATION

Now that you're in management, this is one habit that you need to 86. The consequences of missing a deadline are too serious and costly to your career.

Especially for tasks that require only a few minutes, just do them. Force yourself to get it done and off your to-do list (you DO have a daily to-do list, right?). You will have to force yourself to do it but force yourself. You'll be amazed at how much more you'll get done. Maybe more importantly, is the way you'll feel when you've started early on something (smug, satisfied, cocky, pleased), rather than the way you'll feel if something is late (pathetic, miserable, stressed).

When you find yourself about to procrastinate, fight through it. This is a habit that is difficult to break but you can do it. You've got to get the reputation that when you have a project, task, or duty, it is as good as done. Period. On time, every time.

THE INCREDIBLE PLEASURE OF NOT BEING LATE

Try it. You'll like it.

Even the most motivated managers have some tasks that they just hate and leave for last or never do. Procrastination is learned (and easy) and getting rid of procrastination is also learned (but difficult). In most cases you have trained yourself to procrastinate because you always got away with it before.

But no more. Stop it.

HELP TO GET THINGS DONE AND OFF YOUR PLATE

To-do list. Schedule a specific day and time to work on a task, goal, project, or skill.

Track your progress and celebrate completions. Each time you reach a goal, treat yourself to dinner or buy something you've been putting off getting.

Get Peer Pressure. There's probably another manager who is struggling just like you with a particular skill or project. Go to them, tell them what you're doing and that you'd like to have regular check ins with each other to check the progress each is doing at regular times. Simple but powerful.

Help, I have a question

I am an assistant manager at a restaurant chain. All my servers enjoy talking to one another but sometimes it gets too much when certain servers work the same shift. I usually let it go for 5 minutes before saying something to them to get back to work. The problem is that I'm getting the reputation of making work no fun. Should I let it go on more? Is there a better way to say, "Break it up"? I never say, "Get your butts back to work". Need advice.

Dear Need Advice

You were not hired to make sure everyone is having fun; you were hired to manage a business. But I agree, you also don't want the reputation of being a problem or a jerk. Employees know which managers are jerks, the ones who like to whip out their authority for even the smallest rule infraction. But give your employees credit, they also know which managers truly care about them *and* expect them to do a good job.

You want to come across as both caring and demanding. Managers who just have demanding will fail and those who are just caring will fail. Managers who can combine the two will have employees who want to do a good job, not just be forced to. Remember the old "praise in public but criticize in private"? This also applies here; just take each employee aside and say something like "I know you like to talk to Brandon, but right now let's concentrate on your customers". By taking this tone, I think you'll find that your employees will get the message without taking offense.

Q. If coaching is so great, why do managers avoid coaching?

Common reasons:

- Don't think they have the time

- Fear of confronting an employee with performance criticisms

- Lack of coaching experience, not sure how to do it

CHAPTER 7

THE P&L IS YOUR BFF

First things first

When you first arrive as an assistant manager, ask your GM for copies of the past two or three months of P&L's. (This will probably surprise your GM, since I doubt the GM has ever had that happen before, but don't worry, this is a good thing). You're asking because you want to see how your areas of responsibilities have done over the past few months.

When you get home, go to a quiet place with a yellow highlighter and a pen.

Highlight every single P&L line that is your area of responsibility. Then mark up any areas that were over budget and areas that were super high and needs your immediate attention, starting your next shift.

For example, if you are in charge of the bar, highlight bar labor, including bar training and overtime, bar supplies, Liquor, Beer, and Wine cost of sales, and any other costs that you are personally responsible for.

With this information, you'll get a picture of how well (or badly) your area was managed, at least on the financial side. For the over budget lines, start to get a plan together to figure out what you need to change or do to get those costs lowered. Remember, the P&L is yours now. If you have any questions about anything gray, make a note and ask your GM. The P & L clock is ticking.

BACK TO BASICS

There are three primary financial reports to let managers know what is going on financially: The Balance Sheet, the Profit and Loss Statement (P & L), and the Statement of Cash Flow. Most managers never look at the balance sheet or the statement of cash flows because they don't need them to manage their areas and neither measures their performance. Later, when you are an executive or are buying or selling a business, the others will be vital, but for now, the only one to concentrate on is the P & L.

THIS IS YOUR WORLD NOW

The first step is to speak the language. To be taken seriously, you must be able to understand and use the words and phrases on a P & L. This isn't difficult, but it will seriously help your confidence and impress your GM. Don't say, "You know, the line after you subtract cost of sales", just say Gross Profit. Get in the habit of using the jargon just like your GM.

The next step is to understand where you fit in the restaurant's P&L and finally, being able to put this knowledge to use. The more you get into the P&L, you might be surprised to find that it opens all sorts of doors that are fascinating and essential to running your restaurant.

Do NOT be afraid to ask questions about the P&L. Where did this number come from? How can I make it go up or down? Where do comps go? Why is something this way and not that way? Ask the questions while you're new because later, you'll be expected to know.

Most new managers assume they will not like the accounting part of restaurant management. But you'd be wrong. You'll be surprised that as you start to understand the P & L, you'll find the restaurant comes alive. Do *this* and the P&L responds.

Do *that* and the P&L responds. And, if you let it get away from you, it bites. So, you've got to stay ahead of it and keep it under control. The more you understand it, the better you'll control your area and restaurant.

> If you think you're "no good" in accounting, trust me on this, you'll be right: you'll be no good

Most restaurant managers love instant gratification, I know I did. (Some even say that instant gratification is too slow). The great thing about the P&L is that when you do *anything*, you'll immediately see results on the P&L (good). Total instant gratification. Of course, the opposite is true, when something is wrong and nothing is done to correct the problem, the problem gets worse, and it too shows on the P&L (bad).

The key is realizing that the P&L is a tool that can be your best friend. (Go on, give it a hug. We won't judge). The P&L is a tool so that you can excel as a manager. It points out in black and white the areas where you're good and the areas for improvement.

But first, you must know and understand the P&L. If you are serious about being promoted, you'll embrace the P&L and not fight it. Understanding how to read and work a P&L are essential to becoming a complete manager, ready for promotion.

ARE YOU OVER OR UNDER BUDGET? THAT IS THE QUESTION.

Enter the P&L. The P&L is the tool to figure how the entire restaurant is doing AND it shows in black and white the performance of *each* manager. In other words, it is each manager's report card. You can run, but you can't hide

The P&L summarizes your restaurant's revenues and expenses for a specific period, such as a month, a quarter, or a year and usually compares the current month with an earlier period (For example, this January compared to the prior month or the past January).

A VICIOUS CYCLE TO AVOID

This starts when a manager is over budget. This manager believes the answer to get back in budget is to put in more and more hours which often leads to their performance declining further because they're exhausted. Then they feel guilty for neglecting their family and friends. Then they get incredibly frustrated when their areas are still over budget. Why hasn't all their effort and sacrifice produced results?

The grim reality is this: if your numbers do not improve, all those long hours, sacrifices, and stress mean nothing. Nada. Obviously, this can be a recipe for disaster as the manager works long hours, resentment builds, the family suffers, and performance declines. Very frustrating. Very stressful.

Before all that happens, come up with a plan as soon as you know they're high. Your plan includes logical steps to take to get your costs under control. Then show your plan to the GM for feedback and input. The GM might spot a couple more things that you should do. Your GM wants your costs down just as much as you do!

Make sure you tell your employees that costs are high and you're going to get them lower, but that you'd like their ideas to help.

Results matter, not your effort

AT ITS MOST BASIC

The P&L is like a funnel with sales going into the top, expenses subtracted, and if there are more sales than expenses a profit comes out the bottom. More expenses than sales? A loss.

Sales, revenue, and top line all mean the same thing. Income on the other hand means profit, so never call revenue income or income sales.

THE BUDGET NUMBERS

The budget dollars and percentages are based on how upper management wants to run the business. In other words, upper management looked at the level of customer service, the quality of the product desired, and what level of maintenance and cleanliness is acceptable, then figured what dollars or % of sales the restaurant has to hit to accomplish that. The difference between the *actual* dollars spent compared to the *budget* dollars and percentages (*mainly* percentages) are the basis of what you will be judged on.

WHY BEING UNDER BUDGET CAN BE AS BAD AS BEING OVER BUDGET

If the labor cost was way under budget, it would raise suspicion that staffing was intentionally reduced to cut costs. For example, if you're supposed to have two hosts on, but you only schedule one. Or servers are supposed to have 4 table stations, but you schedule them with 5 table stations. Those would all result in lower customer service to cut costs, or more to the point, management is cutting costs to meet budget.

You are supposed to meet budget fully staffed. Since the budget percentages were based on having two hosts and 4 table stations, it is easy to see the areas where there are questions when the actual percentages are so much lower than budget.

You are responsible whether you are there or not

STARTING AT THE TOP OF THE P&L

Sales and revenue

Sales or revenues (they mean the same) are at the top of the P&L, so it is often called the top line. When a company says they are going after the top line, it means they're trying to increase sales, usually through marketing. Income, on the other hand, means profit and is found at the bottom of the P & L, called the bottom line. When a company says their priority is the bottom line, it usually means they are going to cut costs. Never, ever call sales, income or income, sales.

Sales are from anything that produces well, sales. Sales never include sales tax because your company only collects sales taxes; the company doesn't own it and can't spend it, so it's not included in sales.

Total sales % is always 100%. When you view sales, look for comparisons and trends. For example, if your company put advertising into alcoholic beverages, having alcoholic beverages separated from food would help determine if alcoholic beverage sales go up compared to last month.

Keep in mind that months are not equal. The current month might have had 5 Fridays and Saturdays, while the other had only three. Or one month might be February with only 28 days and the comparison month is March with 31 days. So don't get too excited that sales went up if one of the months had 3 more days or more weekend days.

If the P&L only had sales, it would be of zero help to management. This is because if total sales went up where did it go up? To-go sales? Bar sales? T-shirt sales? Don't know. So, sales are broken out so that management can see which specific areas have gone up or down.

In restaurants, sales are usually split up between meal periods (Breakfast, Lunch, and Dinner) and products (Food, Liquor, Beer, Wine plus any merchandise sales like t-shirts).

Cost of sales is weird

The cost of sales tells how efficient management is in making its products to sell. In restaurants, we sell food and beverages; if you can't eat it or drink it, it is not included in the cost of sales. No straws, glasses, or supplies are included, only the products used to make food or beverages. Typically, non-alcoholic beverages are included in food, while the word beverages usually refer to alcoholic beverages. Cost of sales and labor cost are the two most important costs that can make or break any restaurant.

The purpose of the restaurant cost of sales is to be able to tell which category is causing high food and beverage costs. The more detailed your P&L, the easier it is to pinpoint where a cost is high. Remember, look at and compare using percentages, not dollars. Food other is the broad category that includes everything not in the other food categories, such as canned goods. Bar other includes mixes and garnishes (limes, celery, oranges, etc.)

Here is an example of food and bar costs broken down into categories:	
Meat	Liquor
Seafood	Beer
Produce	Wine
Dairy	Bar other
Bread	Total Bar costs
Other	
Nonalcoholic beverages	
Total food costs	

If the categories only had meat without seafood, if the meat category was it in meat or seafood? Couldn't tell. But when meat and seafood is broken down into separate categories, it would be easy to see which was high.

KEY POINT

To find the percentage cost of produce or bread or any other food cost, divide the $ cost into Total $ FOOD sales, NOT total sales $.

To find the percentage cost of liquor, beer, wine, or bar other, divide the $ cost of each into the $ total bar sales. For example, beer $ into total $ BAR sales, NOT total $ Total Sales.

Dividing food cost or beverage cost into total sales is a very common mistake.

I once consulted to an MD who owned a restaurant but knew nothing at all about owning or running a restaurant. The chef doubled as the general manager. When the doctor contacted me, he said that he had been losing money every month for the past six months since they opened. He said his chef told him this was normal, but he wanted to check this, so he contacted me. When I got to the restaurant, the chef came out wearing the largest toque I had ever seen. He was a big guy anyway, probably 6 feet 8 inches but with his toque, he seemed way over 8 and a half feet tall. Impressive.

Anyway, he sat down with us and immediately said his costs were excellent. Excellent food cost and excellent bar cost; very close to challenging me to prove him wrong.

WELL, OK.

I had reviewed the P&L beforehand and knew the problem. The accounting service that the doctor used was dividing the food cost into total sales and the beverage costs into total sales instead of food costs into food sales and beverage cost into beverage sales. When I pointed this out, and showed him his costs were actually terrible, he realized what had happened. With that out of the way, we could finally work together to lower the high costs.

JUST WRONG

Some managers think they can lower the cost of sales by spending less. This is not even a little bit true. That kind of thinking is why restaurants run out of menu items on the last day of the month because they are trying to get Purchases as low as possible. It does seem to make sense that spending less would result in lower costs. But it doesn't, not with Cost of Sales. However, it does work that way with supplies. So why not cost of sales? Good question. So confusing.

DIFFERENT

The reason is that cost of sales is figured differently than the cost of supplies. The cost of supplies is simple and straight forward. If sales go up, buy more supplies to keep the same percentage. When sales go down, buy less supplies to keep the same percentage. Then divide the total supply cost into total sales and Bang! Supply cost %. Simple.

Cost of sales though, is a completely different animal and is a little more complicated. The good news is that it does make sense if you give it a chance. The biggest difference is that you do not just add up all of the invoices and then divide into sales like supplies or any other expense.

The reason that cost of sales is different than other costs on the P & L is that the cost of sales uses only the money actually spent to produce sales to customers. This means that the money spent on food (or beverages) that are still on your shelves or in cabinets at the end of the month do not count. Only the money spent that made sales to customers.

There's a formula to figure this out.

Wait! Don't turn away. It's not too bad. It even makes sense, so give it a chance.

The formula is:

BI (beginning inventory) + P (Purchases) – EI (ending inventory) = cost of sales

BI is the amount of money spent on food and beverages that were on your shelves, storeroom, or in cabinets at the beginning of the month. To get the real, honest, and actual cost, first get the amount of money that was tied up on your shelves at the beginning of the month (BI), then add in all the money spent on food (or beverages) during the month.

With the total of BI and P, you've now got the entire amount that could have been used for customers. You've got all the food and beverages that you started with plus all the food and beverages that you bought during the month. This amount includes food and beverages that *could* have been stolen, lost, thrown away, spoiled, wasted, discounted to managers and employees, and even food or beverages that were not delivered, but still charged for (ripped off).

Any food or alcoholic beverages that are still on your shelves at the end of the month is simply subtracted from the BI and Purchases. The food and beverages on the shelves (and in the various storerooms or cabinets) are counted and added up making the ending inventory (EI).

The Ending Inventory becomes the Beginning Inventory for the next month

This makes sense when you think about it. The EI is done at the close of the last shift on the last day of the month. No more sales and no more food or drinks will be made that month. This is why the Ending Inventory is used as the Beginning Inventory for the next month (basically the next day).

The only separate Beginning Inventory ever done is the very first one, when the restaurant started. You'll never have to do another separate Beginning Inventory ever again.

THE PAIN OF "DOING INVENTORY"

The good news is that even though there are many costs of sales (one for each category), the actual inventory is done only once. In other words, your goal is to get a % cost of sales for each category (meat, produce, bread, dairy, seafood, food other and liquor, beer, wine, bar other), but thankfully, the physical inventory for all happens at the same time.

The formula (BI + P – EI = COS) is done for each category of food and beverages from the one inventory (YEA!). The Ending Inventory is divided up into its categories (produce, meat, etc and Liquor, beer, etc) and is the Ending Inventory for each particular category.

On the last day of every month, all the managers come back into the restaurant to do inventory. They usually bring coats and a bad attitude. They are probably not in a great mood.

The bad news is that the Ending Inventory has to be done with a physical inventory. This means someone (you) has to be there to count every single item that is edible or drinkable. Each item of meat, seafood, produce, liquor, beer, and all the others must be physically counted. That's why on the last day of each month, all managers are a little bummed. They have to come back into the restaurant, probably around 8 or 9 pm, with coats (going in the walk-in and walk-in freezer is cold!) to do the physical inventory, while one runs the shift.

This is a serious pain in the butt, especially for the day manager who has to come back in and the manager who had the 'day off'. The counts are usually done in teams of two, one counting, the other writing down the counts. Using teams of two is done to be as quick as possible, and so there is less temptation and chance for a manager to cheat.

Since the EI is going to be subtracted from the BI + Purchases, it doesn't matter if you get a truckload delivered on the last day of the month. It has no effect on the cost of sales. The truck load will be added to the Purchases, but the truck load will be subtracted (anything still on the shelves, storeroom, or in cabinets at the time of the inventory will be subtracted, so doesn't matter).

After this, the only thing left to do is to subtract any employee or manager discounts and comps to give a pure cost of sales. These are subtracted from cost of sales so managers are not penalized for giving employees the benefit of discounts. But those discounts and comps are not free. Oh no. These expenses are added to the P&L in another expense category.

DISCOUNTS AND COMPS

Food discounts are a common benefit for employees and managers. Many restaurants give employees working a shift 100% discount (or less) as well as some kind of discount for employees who are not working a shift but come in to eat. If these discounts were not subtracted from the cost of sales, it would raise food costs which would discourage managers from giving discounts. But, because these discounts do not affect cost of sales, managers can give this benefit. This is a really good thing since no one likes a hungry server waiting on them.

WHAT TO DO WITH FOOD PROBLEM AREAS

If some area is high in one area of food costs, the first step would be to go to the storage area to see if any products are out-of-date (you DO make sure every product has a date, right? Right?).

If you see old dates, it means that you are over ordering and probably means your employees have been throwing away old product. The bad news is that a) you're ordering too much and b) they're not telling you. The solution is to redo your par levels ASAP and tell your employees to let you know when anything is out of date or better yet, when it is about to go out of date so you can review your par levels and sales projections.

Your employees want to help and can help, but you've got to let them know you want their help.

1. The next check is to see if you have been ripped off. If one of your employees took even one steak per shift, your cost would be sky high by the end of the month. To put a quick stop to this, count the number of steaks and chicken at the beginning of each shift, subtract out the number sold during the shift, then count again at the end of each shift. The number of meats remaining should equal the number of meats you started with minus the meats sold. Do this at the beginning and end of each shift and you will at the very least know which shift the meat is being stolen from, but most times, stealing will stop. Once you do it a couple of times, this becomes routine, not taking much time at all.

2. Check the invoices that were used to figure out the monthly expenses. Someone could easily have written the wrong number.

3. Lock the walk-ins whenever they are not used for long periods of time like between shifts and at night.

4. Restrict who can go into the walk-ins.

WARNING: The guy who delivers your products knows which managers do a good job checking deliveries and which ones do not. Once they have figured out the managers, you'll be shorted a case. BANG. High costs.

Some managers just check how many total cases are on the invoice, then count to make sure the same number of cases are delivered. Ordered 12 cases, received 12 cases. Perfect.

Ahh but wait grasshopper. Not so quick.

This is not good enough because all cases don't cost the same. If a case of filets is missing, but a case of chicken is one over, the number of cases is correct, but something is wrong in

River City. The most expensive case is missing, and a cheaper case added. Unfortunately, blaming the driver is tough to prove. "Sorry, my screw up". Be careful. The drivers know which managers just count cases.

NOT GOOD

I knew a Food and Beverage director for a large hotel that was just getting open. He was staying at the hotel because he was spending many, many hours each day in the hotel. After a particularly long and tough day, he ordered a bottle of gin brought to his room. After a drink, he put the bottle in the room refrigerator and set it to freezing, so it would be really cold. The next night, he got the bottle out to have a drink, but nothing came out because the gin in the bottle was frozen. Since gin freezes at MINUS 17 degrees Fahrenheit, he knew that at least one bartender was adding water to the gin to make up for giving free drinks away or pocketing the money that should have been rung up. He knew he had work to do.

SHARE THE PROBLEM – DON'T JUST CARRY IT AROUND

Whenever you have a cost problem, it's very (very!) important to tell your employees. When you tell them, be careful to not accuse them, but because you want their help. Telling them helps in two ways. The first lets everyone know that you are aware that costs are high. If one of your employees is stealing, they will probably stop when they realize you know there's a problem. The second reason is to get your employees to help. They can't help if they don't know there's a problem! You'd be surprised at how often they solve problems in just a short time. Getting them involved is key.

Gross Profit is total sales minus total cost of sales. This is the first check to see if you're going to have a good month or bad month. Gross Profit can't tell why you're going to have a good or bad month, only that you did. The only expense that has been subtracted from total sales is the total cost of sales (the cost of both food and beverages).

Sales

  - COS = Gross Profit

  - Operating expenses = Operating Income

Operating expenses. Some restaurant companies call operating expenses controllable expenses because every expense in this section can be controlled by unit management. These expenses all relate to running or operating the restaurant. Usually, the largest expense here is labor costs, but it includes all expenses relating to running the business.

Operating expenses *are* affected by sales, and is why they're also called variable expenses, because the dollar expense varies with sales. This makes sense because the more sales you have, the more costs you'll have. For example, if you normally use 10 servers, and sales go up, you will need more servers. The more customers you have, the more food you'll need. If sales go down, you reduce the number of servers and food that you buy. They are called variable, because the dollars vary with sales. More sales, more dollars. Less sales, less dollars.

Operating expenses include direct and indirect expenses. Direct is just that, labor that is directly used to run the restaurant and each direct labor is in distinct areas (servers, hosts, and bussers are in Dining; cooks, prep and dishwashers are in Kitchen; bartenders are in Bar, etc). Indirect labor benefits the entire restaurant, not just an area, like marketing, accounting, and maintenance. Operating expenses include both employee and management labor, utilities (gas, electricity, water, and internet), supplies, and repairs and maintenance. Operating expenses include all expenses (besides cost of sales) that unit management is responsible for.

As a sidenote, in the US when a shift is slow, managers can often ask employees to go home without paying them. In several countries, Finland for one, once management posts an employee schedule, employees are guaranteed the pay for the entire shift, whether they go home or not. Schedules are taken seriously.

Repairs and Maintenance. These are often grouped together as R & M, but each is different. Repairs cover unexpected expenses (like a broken window) while Maintenance includes scheduled tasks that are performed on a regular basis (like carpet cleaning, window washing, lawn mowing, and others).

Operating income (sometimes called controllable income). Gross profit minus Operating Expenses = Operating Income. This is an important category because this is where many management bonuses are figured. This makes sense since all the expenses above this are completely and totally in management's control.

Total Sales

- COS = Gross Profit

- Operating expenses = Operating Income

- Fixed Expenses = Profit or loss

- Taxes = Net Income

Fixed expenses are expenses that are NOT affected by sales, such as rent, insurance, interest, and depreciation and management have no control of, at least not at the unit level. Fixed expenses stay the same dollar amount each month regardless of sales going up or down. This is one reason why fixed expense budgets are usually given in dollars (rather than %) because their actual dollar amount is known (and doesn't change). Unit managers don't usually pay much attention to this since they can't control them, and they're not judged by them. Upper management gets to worry about this.

Rule of Thumb:

To get the percentage of *any* expense on the P & L, just divide the $ expense into total $ sales.

EXCEPTION: not cost of sales. To get the % of any part of cost of sales, divide the FOOD category into total FOOD sales and divide each Beverage category into total Beverage sales. Never total sales.

Example:

Food sales	$2,000
Beverage sales	$1,000
Total F & B Sales	$3,000
Food Expense	
Meat	$200
Produce	$100
Other	$200
Total food	$500

To get meat expense %.
200 / 2,000 = 10%
If meat expense was divided by total sales, it would be 6.6%

To get total food cost of sales %
500 / 2,000 = 25.0%
If total food cost was divided by total sales, it would be 16.6%

You can see that using total sales gives you much different (and wrong) percentages.

IMPORTANT

Employee schedules are the first budgets that you'll do. Take each schedule you do very seriously. You are approving the amount of money the restaurant will give each employee. You are also having a profound influence on the lives of everyone on your schedule. You have influenced when they do errands, see friends, and can go away on trips. Depending on the shifts you assign, you have influenced how much money they will make. In preparing the schedules, look forward at the sales projections and backwards at the past month, along with last year's month to do your schedules. This is vitally important to hitting your labor budget.

PART THREE
===

PEOPLE, PEOPLE, PEOPLE:

CHAPTER 8

MANAGERS GET THE EMPLOYEES THEY DESERVE

As a manager, you touch the lives of your customers and employees.

Y ou have so many types of employees, some can't read, some can't speak English, some have never had a checking account, while others may be in graduate school.

You'd like to have your employee's loyalty. Easy. Be a caring leader who can show your employees a way to a better life with opportunities and growth. If there is one thing that restaurants *can* offer, it's opportunity for anyone willing to work hard.

Share your knowledge and be honest with them. It doesn't take long for your employees to know which managers they can trust and who deserves their loyalty.

YOUR FIRST ASSIGNMENT / YOUR FIRST RESPONSIBILITY

You've just gotten to be a real, live assistant manager. Congratulations!

You're excited to meet your employees. But, when you ask your GM about them, you're told most are duds. Your job is to shape them up.

Before you get totally bummed out, wait just a minute. What a golden opportunity for you.

Your GM is probably not going to talk badly about the assistant that you are replacing, so you might not ever know what went on. Doesn't matter. You da man right now (male or female).

Think positively. The previous assistant might have ignored the employees and beaten up by a bad manager that they hated. You could be an instant hero.

FIRST AND MOST IMPORTANT STEP

Talk to each employee and get to know them. Be positive. Ask why they are working there. Tell them in your own words that you'll help in any way. Don't be hesitant to give them critical feedback. In my experience, when you give feedback, your personality and caring has a chance to come through. After a while, you'll notice a difference and your GM will be amazed at the turnaround.

IT IS UP TO YOU, THE MANAGER

When employees develop bad attitudes, it's usually management that made them that way. One common reason is that management tolerated bad employees or created a negative environment. You can have excellence in your area.

POWER AND AUTHORITY

They are not the same. Your authority is given to you by upper management through your title and job description. You've got it, you don't need to prove you've got it.

But power is something completely different. Power is on you. Power has to be created. By you. You can gain power by being consistent, by being honest, by being a good manager, knowing more, or being related to the CEO.

SETTING YOUR EMPLOYEES UP FOR SUCCESS

If you've been in management longer than 7 minutes, you know that employees can be one of the most challenging and frustrating parts of your job. But don't get frustrated. Help is on the way. Keep reading.

ENCOURAGE AND RECOGNIZE

If you ever call an employee stupid or tell an employee he or she is bad at something, you've lost that employee. You have destroyed that employee's incentive for ever improving. The better way is to encourage employees. 95% of the time, your encouragement will motivate employees to try to meet your expectations.

Many new managers hate criticizing their employees because they don't like confrontations. I don't blame them; most people don't like to deliver bad news. But don't hesitate to criticize, just do it the right way. As a coach.

The way you deliver criticism is important. Corrective feedback is fine. It's a form of attention that is better than ignoring employees. Corrective feedback is to help, not just to criticize. Constructive criticism is about behavior, not the person.

ENCOURAGE OFTEN

If you're just starting to use encouragement rather than criticism, keep at it. At first, your employees may be confused by your new management style...Who is this manager?

Keep at it and keep at it often. When you see good employee behavior, stop and recognize the employee's behavior. You'll be amazed at how powerful this is and it costs nothing except a moment of your time.

Restaurant management is all about teams. You're trying to have your employees on the same page working together and working to get better.

DIFFERENT STROKES FOR DIFFERENT FOLKS

If you've got a great employee, just ask the employee to do something and they'll do it. *Telling* this type of employee makes this employee resent how they are treated. If done often enough, this will change a great employee into one who resents management and will only do what is in their job description, rather than willingly help managers.

However, for problem employees with write-ups or an attitude, use the direct approach by *telling* these employees.

You'll find that in most situations, coaching is by far the best approach.

A PRETTY GOOD PHILOSOPHY

"Bear" Bryant, the University of Alabama football coaching legend had this approach to teams:
"If anything goes bad, I did it.
If anything goes semi-good, then we did it.
If anything goes really good, then *you* did it."

UNDERSTANDING

Sometimes a little understanding of employee personal problems can have a huge impact. When an employee is not performing well, especially when they were performing well, have a meeting in private, acknowledge the change in performance and simply ask, "What's going on?" That simple question often changes the employee to want to improve when they realize that you've noticed. Your understanding, your simple question wanting to know why their performance changed, can make a world of difference.

THE IMPORTANCE OF HIRING

It is no secret that better employees equal a better life for managers. As a football analogy, hiring an average employee would be like needing 80 yards to score, but when you hire a really good employee, you'd only need 20 yards to score. No brainer to hire the best you can.

Having good employees is not just a function of pay, although good pay certainly helps. If you give unhappy employees more money, you now have unhappy employees with more money.

Few applicants apply for a job with a bad attitude, can't wait to be late, and want to cause problems. New employees **want** to do a good job; they **want** to have a good attitude. It is management's job to keep them that way

---

When you first arrive as the new assistant manager, you're going to be nervous. But your employees are just as nervous about you. Employees know they will have to reestablish themselves with the "new guy". They're going to start from zero with you after they had already "broken in" the last assistant manager. They knew what they could and couldn't do, but now they have no idea what to expect.

As an assistant manager, you are over one department that is your responsibility. As you get to know your employees, make your expectations clear, your standards known, and what you're about. To know more about this, take a look at the chapter on coaching.

CAUTION Be wary of first impressions; give yourself time before you start to think you know your employees. That one employee you thought was a superstar? You may realize later that this employee is a slacker who was just good at sucking up.

ATTITUDE

A great attitude may not be the asset that makes you a great leader, but without a great attitude, you won't go far. It is sometimes tough to keep a great attitude at work, but it is absolutely necessary. The effect of a manager's attitude on others is remarkable. When you show up with a bad attitude, employees feel it instantly and will avoid you, if possible, but worse, their attitudes go down too.

It is important to take responsibility for your attitude. Don't let whatever happens at home prevent you from having a positive attitude at work. You don't want to get the reputation of being moody.

KNOW YOUR EMPLOYEES

Remember they are individuals first, with their own goals, motivations, and reasons for being at work. Some managers forget that and think of them only as "the help", getting to know their employees just enough to know (maybe) their names. That isn't enough. Dig deeper to find out why each employee is working there.

This is super important, because once you know why they're working, you can support them to accomplish whatever it is that makes them come to work, even if it may mean they eventually leave. Besides being fair and consistent, helping them to achieve their goals helps employees trust you and builds loyalty.

What do your employees need to be successful?

Your employees will get a great first impression of you when you come in humbly, ask questions of everyone, and care about your job and their jobs. When your employees realize that you respect them and the jobs they do, they'll tend to do their job the right way, even when you're not there because they feel loyal to you.

When you can make your employees feel recognized and important, you'll succeed.

PERSONAL PROBLEMS

Don't be surprised if you're asked for advice by your employees regarding personal problems. Believe it or not, because you're a manager, you're expected to know the answers to questions about legal, finances, roommates, babies, cars, and relationships. Even if you are single and younger than your employees. I mean, you're the manager, so you know. Right?

It always seemed like a significant portion of my day was spent answering personal problem questions. Don't be surprised if you get 10 questions every day. This is very time consuming, but it's important, so just do the best you can.

CAUTION Some employees will try to draw you in until you feel personally responsible. Keep in mind that it is *their* problem, so back up, you're just trying to help. Do not let yourself get deeply and personally involved. Again, just do the best you can.

YOUR MANAGEMENT STYLE SHOULD BE WITH AN 'S' AT THE END

Gotta have several styles, not style. One size does not fit all. Need to be comfortable with either democratic (asking) or autocratic (telling).

NICE IS NOT NICE

Many new assistant managers think that if they are nice to employees, they will be the best boss in the history of the known world. And by nice, I mean, of course, lenient. You might think this approach will get you great results. The nicer you are to your employees, the more loyal they'll be and the harder they'll work.

Not.

Unfortunately, this style doesn't work and of course, the other end of the spectrum, being the manager from hell, doesn't work either.

But back to nice.

I've come to see this type manager produces several bad side effects. When you are too nice (too lenient), your employees will gradually stretch the rules. They'll arrive later and later, make personal calls, and keep pushing the boundaries until even you have to step in and put a stop to it. Your employees may *like* you, but they won't *respect* you, knowing that you are so nice that they can get away with almost anything. You *will* get burned by your employees and this will hurt.

You're going to ask if their side work is done. They'll tell you 'yes' and later, when everyone has gone home and you're by yourself, you'll actually finally check. SURPRISE! They never did anything. Guess what? *You're* going to have to do the side work. It's late and you're tired. And you're massively pissed.

Unfortunately, when "nice" managers get burned, they tend to do a 180 and go to the opposite of nice: autocratic, stern, a-rule-is-a-rule, by-the-book, don't-take-no-crap-from-no-one, kind of manager. But you'll find that this doesn't work either. You'll get burned again because your employees will resent you and want to make you look bad (and they won't like you!).

No, the best way to manage is by situation, called situational management. Sometimes autocratic (telling) should be used and sometimes nice (asking) should be used. The trick is figuring out when to use the different styles. This was covered extensively in the first book, so I won't bore anyone with repeating it.

Your employees want direction. They want boundaries and they want fairness. If you have a rule, follow them, and enforce them, but do everything with a touch of humanness. I always had exceptions when merited.

ULTIMATUM

I once had an employee who was in high school, helping me with some Excel spreadsheets. One day he comes in and gives me an ultimatum: "My mother said that I should get a raise. I'm doing important work and no one else can do it. If I don't get it, I'm going to have to quit."

I looked at him and said to clock out. I'd do the Excel spreadsheets myself.

I did offer a bit of advice to him. "Don't ever give your boss an ultimatum. Oh, and tell your mother hi".

Ultimatums never end well.

Be friendly, but not a friend

Kids running wild

WHAT WOULD YOU DO?

You are the manager on duty at a full-service restaurant. You're in the kitchen talking to one of your cooks when a server says that a couple at a table has complained about a kid running around disturbing them.

You go out and sure enough, you find a kid about 4 years old running around the dining room. No one else has complained.

SOME CONSIDERATIONS:

• You're sure that other tables are bothered but haven't or won't complain.

• You could go talk to the table and ask them to control their kid.

• If it continues to happen, you could pay for their meal and tell them that they should leave.

• If you must ask them to leave, you risk a scene and a complaint to the GM or corporate.

• If you do nothing, you risk damaging the experience of at least 4 or 5 other tables and a complaint to the GM or corporate.

WHAT TO DO, WHAT TO DO

This is every manager's nightmare basically guaranteeing a lose-lose situation. Somebody is not going to be happy, no matter what you do or don't do. The best thing that a manager can do is find out what the policy is regarding loud or unruly kids BEFORE they run into this situation.

The actions of the manager depend entirely on the company's policy and their attitude towards troublesome kids. Some companies take a hard line, only tolerating one, maybe two warnings before saying adios to the parents. Other companies just leave it to the managers to figure out what to do, so the managers must guess if their actions will be supported or not. I would bet that most managers do nothing when faced with these situations.

You've got to follow policy, so make sure you know the policy backwards and forwards. Then talk the policy over with your GM to make sure the GM and you agree on the actions to take. It is essential that your GM has your back whatever you decide to do: If you decide to comp the meal and ask them to leave or allow the kid to disrupt the other customers and have complaints that you did nothing. Personally, I like policies where restaurant companies do not tolerate kids ruining the meals of other customers. Unless your restaurant is Chuck E. Cheese, they paid money to come to your restaurant to relax not have to put up with kids running around.

CHAPTER 9

COACHING IS NEXT LEVEL

And You're the Coach

OBSTACLE FOR NEW MANAGERS

Keep in mind that each assistant manager is responsible for his/her area. When the income statement comes out, it doesn't care if the manager was there or not there. Your area is your area, every day, whether you are there or not.

Since you can't be at work every single day, employee training and coaching are vitally important.

DIFFERENCE BETWEEN MANAGING AND COACHING

In some ways, managing is easier than coaching. In managing, managers tell, and employees do. At least that's the theory. In managing, the manager directs employees to do tasks for specific purposes. This approach is very effective in the short term, but usually not so great in the long term.

Coaching on the other hand, is more personal, takes more management time and involvement, and is best in the long term, meaning more than a week in restaurant time.

Think of coaching and managing as tools in your tool kit. Once you're comfortable with each tool, you'll know which tool to use in a given situation. Knowing when to direct or coach is critical to your managerial effectiveness.

Managing is more command-and-control style of management, so it should be used when dealing with very new employees, crisis situations, or with problem employees. Make your expectations clear, provide examples, and support so employees can meet or exceed your expectations.

GIVE FEEDBACK

Everyone wants to know the score, even if it is negative. The reason is that when managers engage with employees, even negatively, employees feel noticed and believe that managers are trying to help them do well.

Feedback is *not* just for catching employees doing something wrong and then telling them what they did wrong. Instead, it is about spending a small amount of one-on-one time to get better. Employees totally understand when a manager is helping them as opposed to just telling them they screwed up.

When you give feedback, make it constructive.

- Here's what you did,
- Here's what you should have done,
- Here's why this way is better

THE PROBLEM WITH COACHING

The big problem with coaching is that it takes more time and involvement from management. Sometimes, it can be a giant pain to coach, especially when you're in the middle of something or tired towards the end of the day.

BUT NOT THAT BIG OF A PROBLEM

Coaching should not be thought as dragging yourself over to an employee and spending lots of time that you don't have.

It should take no more than 5 minutes maximum. It is personal and one on one. That's why it is so powerful. When you coach, you'll see a difference in employee attitude and performance in a short time. These changes are because of you. Great job!

Sometimes you'll have to coach and sometimes you'll have to manage. But the more time you spend coaching, the more effective you'll be.

Coaching is a two-part process that involves observation of employee performance and then a conversation between the manager and the employee that focuses on job performance. The goal of coaching is to evaluate work performance and then encourage great work performance by either praising good performance or constructively criticizing poor performance.

Believe it or not, your employees love to be trained and developed because they want to do a great job. They see that you know what goes on and then either praise or critique. You don't ignore them. Your good employees will especially appreciate this while the not-so-good employees will up their game. Plan your training in such a way that it's practical. Explain why you want them to learn the right way in a way that does not talk down to them.

Here's how to coach:

- Speak in private.
- Be specific about the job performance that you observed.
- Actively listen to the employee.
- Focus on the employee's behavior, not the employee.
- Praise or criticize as soon as possible after observing it.
- Be a coach, not a drill sergeant. After coaching, don't stay on someone's back and watch everything they do.

One of the most important reasons that employees, especially our 16 to 22-year old's, stay or leave is because of how they feel about management. If their managers talk down to them, berates them, or humiliates them at work, they're gone. They can and will go somewhere else that treats them better. Just compare turnovers to see that this is true.

To be an outstanding manager, combine directing and coaching. It's not about coaching versus managing, one isn't right and the other wrong, but instead about choosing which one to use in a particular situation. When you can use both, you'll be a much more effective manager.

CHAPTER 10

WE'RE ALL DIFFERENT

Managing older and younger, part-time and full-time

Right now, the U.S. workforce is made up of five different generations, each having very different work experiences, communications, and expectations. Chances are great that you will have older employees, with some being much older.

Some of your older employees will hate having a younger manager and try to ignore you but others won't mind at all, and still others will actually want to mentor you.

When I was a new manager, I worried about not being taken seriously by my older employees. When I was with older employees, I lost confidence in myself, and I became quieter. My GM noticed this change and sat me down.

He said, "Don't ever apologize for your age". Then he asked me a question that really turned it around for me. He asked, "How old do you think you should be to manage your older employees?" I said that I wasn't sure, but probably around 30. He looked at me and said, "OK, you're now 30. Now get back out there and manage like I know you can."

If you're a new manager, here are a few recommendations

Go to older employees first

When you start out, engage your older employees in one-on-ones. Ask them about their experience with the company and what has worked and not worked in the past.

Tell them about your goals for the team and how they fit into those goals. Ask them what support they want and need from you. Tell them you look forward to working with them.

If you treat these interactions with sincerity and not as a task, I guarantee they will appreciate your time and questions. It is a great start to get them to work with you and for you.

PRACTICE BEFORE SPEAKING TO YOUR GROUP

When you first need to speak to your entire team or in a shift meeting, practice. Practice making eye contact, your posture, and showing a positive attitude. Practice helps you speak with confidence and will calm you down.

No one expects you to have all the answers. Be honest about the challenges you expect and your plan to meet those challenges. Finish with a sincere request that you appreciate any feedback or suggestions.

Give credit to your employees whenever possible.
You will gain respect from your employees and your peers.

GET TO KNOW YOUR EMPLOYEES

Learn what is important to your employees. Why did they take the job? What's their best and least favorite parts of work? What rewards or recognitions would be meaningful to them? What is frustrating? The time with your employees will greatly help in establishing you as a manager employees want to work for.

DO NOT COMPROMISE YOUR STANDARDS
JUST TO BE LIKED

Do not be driven by the need to be liked, especially with your older employees. They will see right through this and think of you as weak, greatly hurting your chances of gaining their respect.

PART TIMERS

How do you view your part-time employees? Do you see them as temporary employees who quit at the drop of a hat, have no real interest in their job, and who don't see the "big picture"? If that is the case, then part time morale is going to be an issue and anytime morale is an issue, customer service cannot be at its best.

Most restaurants have its share of part-time employees, but many managers give preference to full-time employees, giving them better shifts with more understanding and tolerance. With their part-timers, some managers can be very policy oriented, black, and white with rules, and intolerant when problems happen.

That is too bad, because they are not only alienating part-time employees with different standards but setting up an attitude in their employees that can encourage negative attitudes towards part time employees resulting in part timers having bad morale, low expectations, and high turnover.

The fact is that part-time employees can be your best employees. After all, they don't usually burn out and they should have the best attitudes since they view the job as necessary to achieve their financial goals or a step toward a career goal.

Some guidelines in dealing with your part-timers:

1. Keep them part time

Honor their schedules. Don't schedule them for more than they said they can work. Even in your worst bind, don't pressure them to work. But, when you do get in a bind, just ask. Don't threaten and don't demand. Most will be glad to help out. Just don't do it regularly; make it the exception. They want to be part timers, so let them be part time.

Make sure that when interviewing, you are specific about future schedules: "Here's the schedule you'll most likely have". Don't set up false expectations that are not realistic. This is probably the number one reason that causes more terminations and ill will than all the others combined with part timers. If in school, they have a social life, classes, homework, and tests to balance with work. If not in school, kids, husbands, wives, or parents require their time and attention. Many times, it is a delicate balance that adding one more shift will be too much, forcing them to leave.

1. Have the same expectations and standards for part-timers as you do with full-time employees

It is essential to be fair and consistent with all rules for everyone. Part-timers will overlook a lot of flaws if they know that everyone is treated the same.

2. They want to feel they are part of the team

Communicate with them. Spend the time to get to know them as individuals and not just a body that you need.

3. Keep it fun

Professionalism and fun can coexist. Big things should be treated as big, but small things should be treated as small.

Part-timers can be some of your best employees. They are usually motivated, eager to come to work, and want to be part of the team. Treat them with respect and as individuals. But most importantly, treat them equally.

CHAPTER 11

TURNING ANGRY CUSTOMERS INTO LOYAL CUSTOMERS

Your behavior determines the behavior you get back from customers

ATTITUDE ADJUSTMENT

The French Laundry, in Yountville, California is one of the best and most expensive restaurants in the United States and in the world. Going there is an event that guests are excited to experience, and have very, very high expectations.

Surprise! Your customers have anticipated going to your restaurant too. They might have brought a friend or family to experience it too. They have high expectations and really, really want your restaurant to meet those expectations.

Keep this in mind when you think of your customers. They have looked forward to coming out to eat all week. At your restaurant. They chose your restaurant. It is up to management to make sure they are not disappointed. Have that attitude for each and every customer.

CUSTOMERS *ARE* THE BIG PICTURE

What do you think of your customers?

- As obstacles that get in the way of your real job?
- Evil necessities in getting your job done?

- Take them for granted and see them as always being there?
- Do you say, only half kidding, "if it weren't for the customers, this would be a great job?"

If the answer is yes to any of the above, there are problems in River City.

First of all, most people, employees and managers, forget what their real job is: to support the customer or support the people who are supporting the customer. It is way too easy to get wrapped up in the details of our job and the self-importance of our jobs, rather than see the real purpose behind all the tasks.

Once you step back and really look at your job, you should be able to see that your real purpose is to serve the customer. It is increasingly easy to view the job as a multitude of tasks and not the more general goal of the customer. We are barraged each minute by orders, phone calls (all urgent), emails, (all urgent), and crises to fix.

In fairness, with all the activities that face the typical manager, it is very easy to think of customers as an interruption in completing the many duties of the job.

It is vital for management to make it clear to everyone that the customer is the bottom line and the reason why tasks are required.

Suggestions for ensuring your employees are customer focused:

- Training is important and ongoing
- Incentives are based on customer service and not strictly on tasks
- Recognition is given to employees who display excellent customer service

- Customer and employee feedback is valued and actively sought

TOUCH TABLES

I often see a manager cruising by tables, slowing down just enough to ask, "Is everything ok?" Most customers answer, "yes, everything's ok". The manager smiles and moves on to the next table because the company policy is to "touch tables".

Personally, I hate this.

Is everything OK? Are you kidding? OK means average, good enough, mediocre, not great, but not bad. Is OK really the standard of your food and service that your company wants? I'd go out on a limb here and say that it isn't.

But your message that you are sending to your customers (and servers and managers) is that OK is what you're shooting for, that OK is good enough.

It isn't.

If you *don't* want average service, maybe you should stop asking if everything is OK unless you really don't want to know the answer to a question like "Is everything fantastic?" When you keep the bar low, you won't be disappointed.

There's a saying "Only mediocre people are always at their best".

Don't let that be you.

Customers are always surprised when
shown excellent customer service

The Trouble with Satisfied Customers.

Does customer satisfaction equal repeat business? Surprisingly, the answer is no.

It can be very frustrating when you're sure your customers are satisfied, but sales are flat or falling. If your feedback from the majority of customers are always positive, what is left to do? I mean, what more can you do than have satisfied customers? Besides the fact that your feedback could be flawed, it could be quite a lot.

To illustrate this, think of your customers as a bell curve with dissatisfied customers on the left end, loyal customers on the right end, and the satisfied majority of customers in the middle.

This entire middle has no loyalty

Customers will switch to another company for almost any reason whether large or small. Maybe the bathroom had towels on the floor, or you were out of a menu item. Regardless of the reason, the vast majority of your customers in the middle can and will go to another company. To change this, establish a connection to your customers in some way.

But be careful. Customers can sense when a manager is not sincere when talking with them. They can tell when an employee does not have the authority to help and they can tell when a server doesn't know the menu.

To build customer service it is necessary to orient, train, develop, and instill a customer service attitude. This begins, of course, with management. Every manager must believe that each employee and product is the best. Each employee must believe that they are the reason that the business is the best.

I'm convinced that your customers *want* to be loyal,
but you have to give them a reason.

Your customers want to feel connected to a particular employee or manager, knowing they will receive good service, or that if a problem happens, they know it will be handled well.

The trouble with satisfied customers is that they just may not show up again. To paraphrase John D. Rockefeller, "The secret of success is to do common things uncommonly well." I think this is one saying that you can take to the bank.

SEEING OPPORTUNITIES, NOT ANNOYANCES

Negative attitudes affect customers. When a customer wants to see you regarding a problem, treat it as an opportunity, not a nuisance.

The first rule of customer service is to believe your customer. Even on the rare occasions when you just know they're trying to scam you, don't let this affect your attitude. Believe them. The vast majority of customers are telling you how they really feel.

When a customer wants to see you regarding a problem,
treat it as an opportunity, not a nuisance.

MOST CUSTOMERS WOULDN'T COMPLAIN IF THEY DIDN'T CARE

Customers know that complaining to a manager can be a process that takes time and could cause a scene, so most totally avoid doing it. So, when you get a customer complaint, treat the complaint with attention and respect. You have a great opportunity to completely change the customer's attitude. I'd bet that many loyal, regular customers started out as disgruntled customers who received exceptional personal care by a manager and employees.

FIX THE PROBLEM THAT CAUSED THE PROBLEM IN THE FIRST PLACE

A good idea is to keep a log of customer complaints so you can recognize problems that happen again and again. You won't notice trends unless you write them down and keep track of them. You'll be able to recognize and eliminate common problems saving you and your employees time and hassle in the future. You want to eliminate these kinds of trends because your goal as a promotable manager is to prevent problems.

CONFRONTATIONS

No one likes confrontations, including managers. It's easy to be intimidated by complaining customers and just want it to end quickly. That's why some managers just go through the motions of helping customers since they just really want it to be over. They think they are obligated to discount or comp whenever they have a customer complaint. At the end, the customer may still not be satisfied, but the manager was able to end the confrontation. The truth is that the manager just didn't want to deal with it.

This is too bad. It is always easier to just do enough to get disgruntled customers out of sight. But to really turn around a bad situation, listen to our customers and hear what they say. Believe it or not, this is the absolute best time for a disgruntled customer to be converted into a loyal customer.

Don't treat a customer complaint as a confrontation. Most customers don't want confrontations either. In many situations, customers just want to be heard by a manager. When a manager sees them and listens, that's all that's required. They just wanted to vent and now that the manager let them, they are satisfied. No discounts or comps needed.

DO YOU EVER NOTICE A MANAGER IN OTHER BUSINESSES?

The next time you're in a restaurant or any business, see if you notice a manager. In most situations, you probably won't. I know I hardly ever do. So, when I notice a manager's presence or a manager stops by, I'm impressed! You may not realize this, but most customers love to know the manager. This is usually a big deal.

Keep in mind that the object is to solve any problem that the customer has. Solving means that both parties are satisfied with the solution. It doesn't always mean you must stick to the letter of company policy, but to make sure your customers leave satisfied, that management was concerned, and solved their problem. This ex-disgruntled customer now knows one of the managers and is now on the way to becoming a regular.

Don't take the easy way out by not talking with customers, because it will only bite you and make the problem worse.

Push yourself and talk to your worst customers. Once you do it a few times, you'll learn that you can be very effective in turning lemons into lemonade. It is a great feeling to know you've made a loyal customer out of someone who potentially would have been lost. Using the direct approach is one aspect of management that will serve you well in your management career.

PART FOUR

NITTY, GRITTY

CHAPTER 12

IF YOU THINK TRAINING ISN'T A BIG DEAL, TRY NOT TRAINING

W eird, isn't it? For equipment, we have preventive maintenance programs, service contracts, and help lines, but after initial employee training, most companies have zip to continue to support their employees.

Your company probably has a commitment to training, designed to get new employees up to speed in as short of time as possible. Customer service, teamwork, and job function skills are drilled into your trainees. They might take tests to show their knowledge of policies and procedures and probably follow trainers for a set number of days before going on to do the job.

Your company may go a step further by requiring trainers to be in-house certified. You are confident that your training is effective and produces employees who are fully qualified from day one.

But many times, they are not.

I have seen too many employees who are just not ready to be by themselves. It might take another chunk of time before they are truly ready to deliver the service that customers expect. I have heard from my students about their training and almost all of them asked a great question: "Who listens to the frustrations of new employees?" Might be time to do some listening.

TRAINING AND LEARNING

- Employees learn at different speeds. Trainers should expect ups and downs of the employees before judging trainees to give them all a chance. Some trainees may look like stars at the beginning of training, then later, they're terrible. Some are so slow at first that you may think about dropping them but wait on these too. Many get better and better until they are the stars by the end of training.

- Learning hardly ever progresses smoothly. Trainees learn with peaks (no problem, I get it) and valleys (I have no clue what I'm doing). Most trainees learn quickest during the first couple of days, then learning slows down.

- Trainees get discouraged. It is very common for trainees to reach a point where he/she isn't improving much or actually getting worse. When that happens, trainees get discouraged. The trainer must be aware of this and give encouragement.

- Nervousness is natural.

- Poor instruction hurts learning. Your trainers should be making the material easy, breaking down anything complicated into smaller pieces, adding humor and the trainer's own experiences to make it more interesting.

SUGGESTIONS TO HELP INSURE EFFECTIVE TRAINING PROGRAMS

1. Get feedback from those just finishing training. After a couple of shifts, have them write down any problems they came across or any questions they had trouble with. Any gaps in their training will be fresh and vivid. If you wait more than a couple of shifts their impressions will be lost. What customer questions did your new employees have trouble answering? What do they feel most unsure of?

Product knowledge? Organizing? Collecting payment? Handling picky customers?

2. Give feedback to trainers. Once you've gotten feedback from the new employees, pass it on to your trainers. Make plans to better incorporate them in future training. This should be done in a cooperative, not accusing way. You're just trying to get better training.

3. Eliminate ineffective trainers. Bad trainers can spoil even the best and most promising trainees. Trainers must be the very best employees you have because they are role models to your new trainees. Bad attitudes give bad attitudes. Do not tolerate bad trainers. Never, ever let an employee be a trainer who has a bad attitude.

4. Evaluate trainer selection and training. Some trainers think they are doing their trainees a favor. Trainers need to be special people who are patient, personable, and knowledgeable. They must enjoy training. They realize that everyone learns at different speeds and give good feedback to their trainees.

5. Recognize and reward your trainers. Make training special. Do something special for your trainers now and then. Great trainers are priceless. Pay them extra, try to give them benefits that no one else has. If your GM agrees, have the GM check with corporate to see if you can make them stand out by wearing something different, such as a different color shirt, or a pin, or something. IMPORTANT: Make sure it is something they want to wear.

6. Be serious about training. Training is the lifeblood of your restaurant. When you find your training lacking, you'll find dissatisfied customers and employees. If you find your training excellent, you'll find satisfied employees and customers.

Remember that your employees represent your company and you to the public. By completing training, you have given your endorsement that they are ready. Make sure they are.

STAGES OF TRAINING

Tell. Show. Do. Review. Repeat.

Tell. Show. Do. Review. Repeat.

You get the idea.

CHAPTER 13

MOTIVATING

It's not always about the money

MOTIVATING EMPLOYEES

There's an interesting study that asked employees what they wanted most from their jobs. This same study also asked managers what they thought employees wanted most from their jobs.

Predictably, managers answered that they thought employees most cared about money. Then job security, then promotion opportunities.

The really interesting fact is that employees found that money wasn't even in the top 3. They most cared about feeling appreciated for the work they do, feeling "in" on things, and sympathetic help with personal problems.

See the disconnect here? How can you successfully manage and motivate your employees if you don't even know what motivates them? There is a serious problem here that makes motivating so much tougher than it has to be. When managers think that money is the prime motivator when the reality is just showing appreciation is the real motivator, can only cause frustration for both managers and employees, leading to bad morale, and eventual turnover.

Showing that you care costs nothing but can motivate your employees to do a great job for the right reasons. They will do a great job for you because it's personal now. I mean who doesn't like an "attaboy", especially when it comes from someone who actually cares about you?

Managers who believe that employees are only interested in more money severely limits their ability to establish a personal connection and manage effectively.

CARE

A more powerful way to motivate is to care about your employees. You do this by taking a sincere interest in what they want from their jobs and do everything you can to help them achieve their goals. For example, if they are interested in getting into management, attempt to give them added responsibilities, or cross training, or assign a project to them so that they can get noticed by the GM.

If they're struggling with English, explore classes in English as a Second Language. These are usually free or at a nominal expense. Don't forget to add transportation costs and flexible schedules to accommodate classes.

If they are in school, work around their school schedules, exams, and projects. If they are trying to pay their bills, try to give them a steady schedule and maximum hours.

When your employees realize that you are sincere in wanting to help them in their development and goals, you'll be amazed at the difference. Motivating works best when it is personal.

What qualities of a job are important to your employees? I'm sure feeling included, informed, respected, a sense that they can 'make a difference', benefits, bonuses, promotion opportunities, money and recognition, all come to mind.

These are all important aspects in a job, but one that I think is even more important but receives little notice is job security. When it is absent, it is overwhelming and makes all other qualities of a job unimportant.

There are many, many employees in the world who live in constant fear of their jobs because their manager manages by fear. Fear is effective because people tend to do what they're told when threats are used. Most employees (and managers) cannot handle being greeted everyday with "I'm watching you" or "I'm going to get you fired".

This way is effective, but there is a price to pay for this 'effectiveness'. When job security is missing, it will be replaced with doubts, defensiveness, and a feeling of low self-worth.

Employees will begin to close up, get defensive, and work defensively, trying to make as few mistakes as possible to avoid the wrath of their manager.

After a while, it becomes apparent that the job is not worth the price of feeling threatened and defensive each day and they eventually quit. I don't blame them.

But what makes this worse is that these 'quits' will probably go unnoticed. The GM's boss might ask why the employees quit and will get something like "oh, he was just burned out" or "She realized that this job wasn't for her" and the subject will be dropped.

The result of this type of manager is high employee turnover, low morale, inferior customer service, and high cost of recruiting, hiring, and training new employees, plus the huge toll on managers. Hopefully, your GM will notice.

RECOGNITION

The great thing about recognizing your employees is that it so powerful and doesn't affect your P&L in any way; yet a simple "good job" is so powerful. It sends a strong message that you "see" them and took the time to personally praise the employee. Powerful stuff and the price is right too. I guarantee that they'll tell their significant other later, and they'll also tell their peers. Your stock just went way up.

RESPECT

Respect is a powerful motivator. So many employees do not feel respected or seen, with many feeling like they are "the help". When employees feel they are just bodies filling spaces, with no respect for them or their job, it is not surprising that the quality of their work and their loyalty will not be there.

GETTING TO T-E-A-M-W-O-R-K

Customer service has many components, not the least of which is teamwork. When a restaurant has teamwork, it is a thing of beauty. Hot food delivered hot, cold food cold, and employees know their area will be covered in case they get busy elsewhere. No one worries about doing more than their share or someone slacking. Employees have confidence in their managers to keep all the areas stocked and staffed so that they can best serve their guests. Employees have confidence that their managers will notice problems quickly so that they can be prevented from becoming serious.

But the age-old question is how? *How* does a manager get this elusive teamwork started in their area? Do they enforce teamwork with "EVERYONE WILL...!" Or "Anyone NOT doing X will be given a write-up!" Does that really develop teamwork?

Maybe posting signs like "BE KIND to each other! Show RESPECT! Don't YELL! You MUST say PLEASE and THANK YOU!"

They'll work all right, but only if the manager is around. As soon as the manager leaves the area, employees roll their eyes and immediately return to their old behaviors.

Teamwork cannot be forced.

Trying to force teamwork damages morale and hurts your credibility.

When employees don't believe it, they don't do it

The true, acid test of real behavior is to observe employee behavior when there is no manager watching them. What do they do on their own when there will be no reward or punishment? You can bet that management has been successful when employees are doing a great job when no one is looking.

To help develop teamwork you should consistently:

- Ask if there is anything that you can do (and mean it). Then do it

- Be involved, circulate, and know what is going on in the restaurant

- Never get bogged down in crisis management (putting out small fires, while the business burns down)

- Lead by example in attitude, behavior, and actions

- Notice and praise employees for doing "teamwork" type behavior

- Notice and reprimand employees who do not do "teamwork" type behavior

- Do not tolerate employees who consistently resist teamwork
- Keep your attitude even and positive

When employees know this type of manager is on, the shift runs smoother. When all the managers have this same philosophy, teamwork flows, turnover slows, and customer service improves.

Some suggestions to make employees feel like they make a difference:

ASK FOR SUGGESTIONS ON WHAT NEEDS TO BE CHANGED

Employees know their jobs and they can improve their jobs. But here's the thing: no one ever asks them!

So, want to help your credibility? Ask each employee if they have any ideas as to how any part of their job could be made easier, cause less waste, or go faster. I guarantee you'll get some great ideas.

Share the good suggestions with your GM. Ask the GM to personally thank that employee. Don't worry, you'll still get massive credit, but you'll also get a heavy dose of loyalty from the employee. They will tell other employees about how you actually told the GM that the employee had a good idea.

Note: if you do implement any suggestion, make sure to tell the employee. If you just go ahead and make changes without telling them, you have wasted a great opportunity and they'll resent you big time.

PRAISE!

Celebrate milestones, events, look for things to praise at shift meetings. This is why it is so important to get to know each employee on an individual basis. If you want to give them something, make sure that something has meaning.

BE CUSTOMER DRIVEN

Allow some freedom to use their own judgement concerning minor customer requests or complaints. Check with your GM about this.

COMMUNICATE

Let your employees know what is going on in shift meetings. For an example, they shouldn't find out that their uniform is going to change the next day when management has known about it for weeks.

REALISTIC JOB EVALS

Have clear expectations that you have explained in advance. No surprises or vague expectations.

GIVE CHANCE TO GROW AND LEARN

Some employees get burnt out by doing the same job day in and day out for years. One thing you might do is to offer to cross train them. With the GM's approval, you might also pay for taking relevant courses at the community college like a wine class.

Sometimes, really good employees get bored or be on the verge of getting burned out. They just might be ready to get into management, something the employee might not even have considered. Talk to your GM first about the employee and if the GM agrees, don't hesitate to float it by the employee. You never know, you might have launched a management career.

EMPLOYEES DON'T START THEIR DAY WITH A DESIRE TO GET BEAT UP

Most employees start the day enthusiastically. Your job is to keep those enthusiastic fires burning.

IMPORTANT Employees want to know the rules and they want everyone to follow them. This means fair and consistent rules. Weak managers, who just can't or won't give negative feedback, or managers who give special treatment to their favorite employees, can never gain employee respect and can never be promotable managers.

CHAPTER 14

MICROMANAGING

Good leadership is About Letting go

Micromanagement is exactly what it sounds like; managers who try to control everything, even the smallest details. Some new managers might even admit to being control freaks, as a point of pride, like that somehow excuses their behavior. It does not. But I get it. It's totally understandable for a new manager to get into micromanagement since he/she wants everything to go well.

Being a control freak/micromanager is not a good thing. In fact, it is a very bad thing.

WHY MICROMANAGE?

The most common reason and a really good one, is that new managers are trying to establish their reputations and want their first assignments to go really well. It seems logical that they should be hyper involved, otherwise projects might not go well and reflect badly on them. Totally true.

But.

Experience and research show that employees who are micromanaged perform poorly. So, while you might think that micromanaging guarantees great results and you'll look like the star that you are, you'll actually be hurting your area and working much harder than you need to.

Micromanaging managers tend to produce employees who are disengaged, stressed, have low productivity, and who burn out quickly.

Micromanagement is *not* working smarter.

OK. So, what do I do?

You can give your employees some space; in other words, start to trust them.

New managers often think that their area will completely go to hell the minute they're not around. This may be true with a few employees, but most will welcome not being constantly harassed (their view) or checked on (your view).

EASE OFF AND BEGIN TO TRUST

At first, you might have a hard time trusting your employees to do their jobs in a timely and quality way. Sometimes new managers even believe they can do some tasks better. This is probably not true. But even if it were true, that's not your job, managing is. Don't allow yourself to get stuck down in the weeds.

To ease out of micromanaging, figure out who your worst performing employees are and who your good ones are. With your good employees, start to ease up, and as you begin to trust them, ease up even more. Just tell them if they need help, just ask. They'll appreciate it. With the poorer performing employees, continue close supervision and, since you have more time, attempt to coach them.

Provide clear expectations and then trust your employees to do what's expected of them. This is difficult at first, but once you know who to leave alone and who requires supervision, your job will be so much easier. It's an old truism that 80% of management time is spent on the worst 20% of employees. This should help to ease that up.

IF YOU'RE GUILTY OF MICROMANAGING, TRY THIS

One of the worst aspects of micromanaging is that it takes so much of your time. And most of the micromanaging that you're doing is completely unproductive. As a manager, focus on planning and preparation, not the small things. When you eliminate the petty stuff that you don't need to get involved in, you'll be able to double your management productivity and effectiveness. Don't criticize employees when they take initiative. You want initiative. When you're too quick to criticize, you're training your employees to get your permission first. This is time consuming and unproductive for you, but even more frustrating for the employees. And, oh yeah, the customers. Your employees will go completely defensive, trying not to screw up and never again take any initiative because you have trained them that you won't like what they did.

IT'S ALL ABOUT THE ENVIRONMENT

Promotable managers create an environment where employees can learn from their mistakes, rather than walk around on eggshells trying not to screw up.

Promotable managers want input from their employees and should encourage input. You just might be surprised at how much your employees know and want to share if only they had a manager who was secure enough to listen.

Each of your employees have very different experiences and perspectives than you. Encourage their opinions; listen, and, if you use any of their ideas, make sure you tell them and give them credit. You'll be a much better manager and will begin to gain their trust.

TALK TO YOUR TEAM

To get away from micromanaging, stop and plan. What are your priorities? Rank these priorities. Which ones do you have to personally do? Which ones could you delegate? Once you do this, communicate your plan with reasons why your plan will work. This is an important step because it is vital to get buy-in from your employees. Be patient, spend whatever time is needed, and ask if there are any questions.

Make sure you let them know that you have faith in their abilities. If things don't go exactly as you'd like, coach, don't go ballistic. You'll be amazed at how effective you'll be and how productive they'll be.

Your job as a promotable manager is to be part manager and part leader: Managing is planning, while leading creates employee buy-in

---

CHAPTER 15

DELEGATING

Your best friend and superpower

D on't just do it yourself. Try delegating. Most new managers either hate to delegate or *really* hate to delegate because of one of two reasons:

1. If I don't do it, it won't get done, or won't get done right

2. If someone else does it, I won't get credit for doing it.

Both are totally wrong.

REALITY OF YOUR NEW ROLE

As an employee, you drove the bus trying to be the best driver possible. But in management, you're no longer driving, you're in the back seat. Your success now comes from and through your employees. Your employees and area must be the success, not just you. After so long trying to be the best individually, it takes a reset to grasp that you must help others succeed for you to succeed.

This is a difficult transition. Now that you're the head of a team, you *cannot* do it all yourself.

New managers are given huge amounts of responsibilities, deadlines, and pressure to meet those responsibilities. Most new managers push themselves because they got into management by excelling as individuals. The stress for new managers can sometimes be devastating, sometimes resulting in managers quitting. Too much, too soon. This is unfortunate since delegating could go a long way to help that. Unfortunately, some new managers often don't even consider delegating.

DELEGATING IS HARD

Delegation doesn't seem to be difficult but may actually be one of the most difficult tasks for new managers. Often, they'll hesitate to delegate because they worry that they won't get credit. This is totally understandable since new managers are working for early wins and credit for those wins.

Sometimes, new managers don't think employees will do a good job. Because of that fear, they tend to smother employees with close supervision, frustrating employees. Sometimes new managers think that team members will resent new tasks added to their normal responsibilities, but the truth is that when done right, delegating is your best friend and can help employees by offering them opportunities to shine that could lead to their advancement if they want or maybe just extra hours.

YOUR NEW ROLE

You are no longer acting as an individual.

A management fact of life:
You've got to delegate.
You simply cannot get everything done if you don't delegate.

It is a matter of being productive. Your general manager must delegate and your regional manager delegates even more. The higher you go in management, the more you delegate.

Any worries about not getting credit are just wrong because your GM is interested in results. As long as the job, project, or task gets done, you get all the credit for it, no matter who actually does it.

ALWAYS GIVE CREDIT

Make sure you give credit to employees who did the job to your GM. This will go a long way in making them feel recognized and valued and help gain their trust. Win-win.

Delegation is a significant way to develop your employees. This is exactly how you and the other assistants are getting developed. You'll be surprised at how many are willing and motivated to accept more responsibility, but it is up to you to give them this chance. You'll find it is one of the most satisfying parts of your job as manager.

When you get bogged down in detail stuff, you're not helping yourself or your area. You might feel pretty good about getting involved, but what's happening to the rest of your area? Probably going to hell and for no reason.

What if there was an incident that happened at that exact time? Could people find you in time to help? Managers should not allow themselves to get tied down to one area so they cannot manage the restaurant.

Once you understand delegation and start to incorporate it into your daily management routine, you'll find your own efficiency and productivity takes a quantum leap forward. Fasten your seatbelts ladies and gentlemen, we have lift off.

GO FROM DOING TO LEADING

You've got a shift to run, but you also want to accomplish your weekly goals. What to do?

Delegate of course.

The best part of delegation is that you are able to run a good shift while accomplishing a project or task at the same time. How good is that?

One of the most difficult transitions for managers is to go from doing to leading. As a new manager you cannot be successful by holding on to what you used to do. It is one thing to help out, to be a role model, and to show that you are not too good to do work. But you'll learn that your responsibilities do not allow you to become too involved in your employee's work.

You will be able to increase your effectiveness only when you stop thinking like an employee and understand that an effective manager allows their employees to do their jobs. Otherwise, your GM will always see you as an employee and never see you as an experienced manager. Holding on to employee tasks limits your ability to get your goals accomplished. This is tough for new managers because it seems like you're giving up some of your authority. You're not.

Just as being busy is not the same as being productive, doing employee tasks is not the same as managing.

WHEN YOU DELEGATE

Who do you delegate to?

The employee you select to delegate is important. Do NOT just grab the first employee and tell the employee this is what they are going to do. I usually chose either a really good employee who wanted some extra hours or an employee who wanted to get into management. I would also give them a free meal to sweeten the deal.

Make sure you explain to the employee what you want done and that they understand. It sounds tired, but have the employee repeat back to you what it is they are going to do. This eliminates a lot of problems. And, maybe most importantly, make sure you check back to make sure everything is going the way you expect it to go.

Tell them why. When employees are only told what to do with no context about why they're doing it, the chances of them buying in are zero. To get buy-in, tell them you're having them do it.

Show confidence in them. Employees love to know that their manager has confidence in them. Once you have communicated the job and your expectations, tell them you'll check on them later, and let you know if they have any questions.

They can't read your mind. It is the responsibility of the speaker (you!), not the listener, to make sure that information is clear and understood. It never hurts to have them tell you back in their own words what you said regarding the job and your expectations.

THE RESPONSIBILITY IS STILL ALL YOURS

It is ultra-important that you realize that your responsibility does not end when you delegate. It is still all yours. If the project winds up going to hell, it is still your responsibility. You can never, ever use the excuse that you told them what to do. You have no excuses. That's why you've got to be clear and check back often.

Limited supervision. It's essential to stay involved, but not too much and not too little. Too much is counterproductive of your time and frustrating to your employees. Too little may result in the job not done as you wanted or expected.

You will get all the praise for getting tasks done right, but you will also justifiably receive all the blame if it goes wrong. This is totally on you. That is why choosing the right person, explaining exactly what needs to be done, and periodically checking on progress with corrections as needed, are all essential.

Finally, make sure you thank the employee and tell the GM how good the employee did. Win – win. You get credit for getting your project done and your employee gets the extra hours that he or she wanted. I almost always included a meal to sweeten the deal.

> **WARNING** Be careful not to keep going to the same employee. If you ask the same employee over and over, they will feel used no matter what incentives are offered.
> Delegating allows development of yourself and others. Delegating gets you ready for promotion and lets your GM see you developing others.

CHAPTER 16

WHEN YOU JUST HAVE TO DISCIPLINE, REPRIMAND, OR TERMINATE

Firing is always the last resort, but sometimes you gotta do what you gotta do

I t's always tough to terminate an employee. And it should be tough.

I am a believer that when employees are screwing up so much that you think about firing them, there must be something going on with them.

Restaurant managers are a caring sort, really wanting what is best for their employees, so we often tend to ease things over and sugar coat issues. But you'll be surprised that people really do want the truth.

When an employee under performs, sit them down in private, then ask if they like what they do. When you think about it, isn't it impossible to be good at anything that you hate? If (or when) they admit they are miserable in their job, try to find out why. It might have nothing to do with you, other managers, or the job at all. It could be financial, personal, or family problems, all far from work problems.

If they open up to you about what is really happening to them, you might be able to turn them around simply by trying to understand where they are coming from.

However, if they just hate the job or management, remind them that they will hate it even more next week, and even more the week after that. Why stay miserable? Encourage them that it might be best to move on to another job or even another industry. So, on the rare occasions that you must terminate, you're really releasing them from a kind of prison. After talking it through, most realize that it is a mutual decision, not just being terminated.

People who don't like what they do are destined to fail. Life is too short to work where you hate. In the long run, you'll be doing them and your company a favor.

Should you keep trying with your worst employees?

The answer is yes, you should try. But, when you've tried, that's it. You may think you're doing the right thing by continuing to work with them, but what you are really doing is bringing your best people down and making a ton more work for yourself. Obviously, you can't keep doing this. You've tried, now it's time to cut bait.

Hire fast. Fire slow.

Before you even think about terminating an employee:

Four words:

Document. Document. Document. Document.

DOCUMENT BOTH ORAL AND WRITTEN WARNINGS

Even though documenting an oral warning sounds like an oxymoron, you've got to write it down. Otherwise, how would another manager know that an employee got an oral warning? Usually, a company has some kind of policy that says that after three *written* warnings an employee can be terminated. The oral warning does not count for an official strike against the employee, but it does alert the employee (and management) that whatever he or she is doing, needs to stop.

REVIEW PAST PERFORMANCE REVIEWS AND WARNINGS

Before you go to the GM to say that you'd like to terminate someone, take a look at their past reviews and any oral and written warnings. As a new assistant, you probably don't know the GM all that well. I suggest you pause if you find the employee has only received positive reviews. Something's wrong. Why is there such a difference between how you think the employee is doing and what *other* managers think of the employee? Is it you or is it the employee? Has something changed? Seek advice from your GM and other managers who know this employee.

The goal of employee performance reviews is to set goals and expectations and to review how those expectations were met or not met. They also help protect your company when reviews show that the employee knew the company's performance standards and did not meet those standards.

NEVER A SURPRISE TO THE EMPLOYEE

An employee should never be surprised at being terminated. There should be warnings and performance reviews that lay out a pattern of poor performance. Follow your human resources guidelines.

The exception is for employees who violate serious policies. Don't wait, they should be terminated immediately. Make sure you know what those serious policies are.

ALWAYS IN PRIVATE AND IN PERSON

Always fire in private, never in public.

If the employee is known to be difficult, always have another manager with you.

Firing an employee should never be by phone, email, or text. While the experience will never be pleasant, it should always be professional.

KEEP IT SHORT AND PROFESSIONAL

When it's time to fire someone, avoid small talk and get straight to the point. Tell the person directly that he or she has been terminated. Employees will often give reasons why they should not be fired. Make it clear that this decision is final and give specific reasons why this decision was made (past performance reviews, oral and written warnings, etc). No hesitation, say firmly that this decision is final.

After you tell them, ask them if they have any questions regarding their last paycheck or benefits.

RESTRICT EMPLOYEE ACCESS

If the employee had a key to the building or office, change the locks. If the employee has company email, alert IT or HR that the employee should no longer have access.

GET THE WORD OUT

While the best approach may seem like keeping quiet about terminations once they have happened, it is not. If employees ask, it's best to be honest. If you don't, your employees will hear all sorts of rumors. You don't have to say why he doesn't work there anymore, only that he doesn't.

PART FIVE

TO BE A GREAT #1, YOU'VE GOT TO BE A GREAT #2

CHAPTER 17

TO BE A GREAT #1, YOU'VE GOT TO BE A GREAT #2

In a restaurant chain, you're all serving the same food, using the same systems, all within similar buildings. So, what makes each different?

Management. Management makes the difference, and this means you.

Studies comparing assistant managers who got fired with those who got promotions revealed a common denominator in each one. The assistant managers whose careers got hurt did not develop. They stayed with their initial strengths but failed to develop more. For example, they were hands-on or were very good at one thing (cooking, bartending, attention to detail, shifts, POS, etc.). These initial strengths became fatal flaws later, because they could not or did not adapt to their new levels of responsibility, like going from employee to assistant manager or from assistant manager to GM.

When you first get promoted to assistant manager, your role changes. You job is no longer about personal achievement but instead about enabling others to achieve.

SO WHY DO SOME ASSISTANT MANAGERS GET PROMOTED OVER OTHERS?

By doing a great job each shift, so you're ready when a promotion opportunity arises. Keep yourself positioned so that timing is always right for you.

THE ESSENTIAL MANAGEMENT SKILLS:

Delegating

Rookie managers tend to "just do it" because they fear losing control. Failure to delegate limits their own productivity and can block their employees' advancement.

Ask for help

It's OK to not know, but when you don't know, ask for help. You want your employees to ask for your help if they don't know something. You do the same.

Never, ever, never cover up a problem. Fess up and ask for help.

Try to meet other managers as resources for each other.

Project confidence

Be aware of your image. It is impossible to project yourself as promotable if you are frantic, arrogant, or insecure.

Preventive management

Resist crisis management. Putting out fires feels productive, but it isn't. Concentrate on preventive management.

Give constructive feedback

Most rookie managers dread correcting their employees. But if you avoid doing it, you damage your credibility.

EVERYTHING YOU DO OR SAY MATTERS

You just might be amazed if you could hear what your employees say after you meet with them. You just might be shocked to find that your words really did matter. Just by being a manager, your words and actions matter a great deal.

Every single thing you say and do matters much more than you think it does. One piece of advice: If your GM could hear what you are saying, would you say it? If the answer is yes, go right ahead. If the answer is no, stop now.

Every email you send, the way you look each day, your posture, your mood, your focus, is a reflection of you. Keep this in mind when you are tempted to slack off. Because, naturally, that will be the day that your GM's boss will visit to check you out after all the great things your GM has said about you. Your impression will not be impressive, and a great opportunity will be lost.

Act the part. Look the part. Do the part.

CRITICAL REFLECTION

After a tough shift, do you say "wow, that was a tough shift, let's go get a beer" or do you take a moment to reflect on why it was a tough shift? It is important in your development to reflect on the whys and what you could do differently.

What can I learn from that? How would I set it up differently so that I get a better result? Talk with your GM when you have a tough shift. I think most GMs appreciate that you want to learn from them.

QUICKIES:

PRACTICE REQUIRED

It is difficult to be a complete manager ready for promotion, so more reflection is necessary. What are you good at and what are you not particularly good at? To use a sports analogy, if you play baseball, and you're really good at hitting, but suck at fielding, you're going to have to spend more time practicing fielding. Managers are the same. If you hate dealing with customer complaints, or struggle with administration, or one of hundreds of skills that you need to be promotable, you're going to have to focus in on getting better at those. To be promotable, you need strong administration skills, P&L smarts, and good human relation skills. Make a list of what you're not great at and get to work.

IT'S NOT ABOUT YOU

At the end of the day, it is not about you. It is about your employees and your customers. When you understand and buy in to that, you'll be on your way to being promoted.

FOLLOW THROUGH

To get a great reputation, one of the most important, expected, and basic parts of your job is to gain the trust of your GM and your fellow assistants. One way to do this is that once you say you'll do something, it is done. If something stands in your way, first try to solve it yourself, but if you can't, go immediately to your GM for assistance. Don't ever look at something you've done and say "Well, it's better than it was". Do it completely right like you would want your assistants to do when you're GM.

THE "OTHER GUY"

Excuses are for managers who are not going to be promoted. Promotable managers are always in control of situations. Excuses are for "the other guy". Making an excuse is the same thing as saying that another manager would have done the same thing. "I was 20 minutes late because traffic was really bad". "I did everything I could, but the customers still left mad".

Be careful with excuses, they almost always (always) make you look bad. Here's how: Another manager would have anticipated traffic and left earlier. Another manager would have found a way to have the customers' leave with a positive experience.

YOUR GM LOOKS GOOD, YOU LOOK GOOD

It is important to pay attention to opportunities that come along when your GM could use some help. This is not playing up to the GM, it is simply helping your career by helping a team member who can also help you. I have never seen a GM who forgot when an assistant manager put in extra effort to help them. It may not help you immediately, but you are planting a seed that could be invaluable one day.

TAKE GRUNT WORK OFF YOUR GM'S HANDS

Be aware of what your GM hates doing. I had one GM who hated to place produce orders. So, I always did it when I had the chance. I'd just mention it in passing, no big deal, but I knew the GM appreciated it.

The GM may hate something that's time consuming, difficult, or the GM just hates. This is the perfect opportunity to say, "I'll take that". If you do this, make sure you do a great job. This is one more way to differentiate yourself from the other assistants.

OWN IT

If or when you have to defend a corporate policy at a shift meeting, don't undermine your own authority by falling back with "this is what management wants". You must be persuasive to your employees that you own it, that you're not just delivering a message.

Whenever a new procedure, menu item, or rule, is beginning, ask the GM questions and get your criticisms off your chest. But once you've done all that, that's it. Don't continue to question the GM about the wisdom of the procedure and don't express any doubts to your employees.

You'll find that a company can roll out a bad idea, but do a great job rolling it out, and your employees will buy in. But if a company rolls out a great idea poorly, it will fail. You do not want to be the reason it fails. Buying in and owning it are key. Occasionally, this is tough on you if you really disagree, but get over it. Own it.

IT'S A PARTNERSHIP

Some new managers see their role as submissive to the GM, rather than as a partnership. They don't initiate meetings, question results, or ask for guidance because of two reasons. One is that the GM intimidates them and the second is that they think that asking questions seems like a weakness. Neither is correct. Do initiate, do ask questions, and do ask for guidance.

BE IN A GOOD MOOD

Be in a good mood with positive energy and be passionate about your job. These will flow through you to each employee who will in turn show this energy to the customers.

LISTEN TO YOUR EMPLOYEES

Get to know each employee and listen to them. Go ahead and initiate conversations, don't wait for them. You'll probably find out there are true stars on your team who have gone unnoticed.

DIFFICULT CONVERSATIONS

Sometimes you just have to have difficult conversations with your employees. Don't be afraid of them but do approach them in a meaningful way. Have professional, not personal, honest talks with them.

ACCOUNTABLE

Never hold your employees accountable for anything you have not told them.

EASY CHOICE

You're overloaded with hundreds of priority stuff to do. An employee stops by to tell you the bar is out of olives. Easy choice. You go get the olives. Your employees are always your priority.

YOUR JOB

Your job is to make your staff better. Your ability to develop employees is essential to be promotable.

YIN AND YANG

For every 5 employee sit-downs to discuss problems, have 5 sit-downs to discuss employee successes.

NOTHING TO PROVE

You're the manager. You're in charge. Your employees know you're in charge. You've got nothing to prove to your employees. Stay humble, listen to your employees. It costs nothing to listen to complaints or suggestions. You'll always get better results when employees are on your side.

LIKED OR RESPECTED?

They're not mutually exclusive. You can have both. When you listen and treat your employees well, your employees will both respect and like.

THANK YOU

You should say thank you more than any other words on your shift. Appreciation is powerful and costs nothing.

FOCUS

Keep in mind what is most important to you by using your career plan. This prevents you from getting distracted and tempted from changing jobs for the wrong reasons. This happened to me when I took a detour from the path that I knew was right and wound up costing me a lot of time and stress.

The weather was bad with snow and ice on the ground making it extremely slippery.
My friend and I were walking back to my car when I almost slipped on the ice. I started to walk even more carefully, trying not to fall. A few minutes later, I heard my friend yell at me. I had walked right by the car for a couple of minutes.
My friend had kept the objective to 'get to the car', but my focus had shifted to 'not slipping'. I was doing a great job of not slipping, but I had totally lost my primary focus, that of *finding the car*.

KEEP LEARNING, GROWING, AND DEVELOPING

- Read a management book (the One Minute Manager by Ken Blanchard is one of my all-time favorites)
- Attend a workshop
- Take a course
- Get a certification

PERSONAL PR

Take advantage of any opportunity to interact with your GM's boss.

For example, if you go to a Christmas party where key people are attending, go over and talk to them. They're often standing alone because managers feel awkward approaching them. Ask their opinion on industry news or trends that you've been reading about. (You are reading about restaurant trends and news, aren't you?). But, never, ever, never, put them on the spot by asking about company matters such as, "Is it true that the GM will be transferring next month?".

MYTH: I SHOULDN'T HAVE TO ASK FOR A PROMOTION

Actually, yes you do. Kind of. You believe that your GM knows who is doing a great job and who isn't. You're absolutely sure that when the GM knows of a promotion opportunity, the GM will support you because you have worked your tail off and you deserve it. You may even believe that if you have to ask, you don't deserve it, that you're begging.

REALITY: THE SQUEAKY WHEEL DOES GET THE GREASE

There are a million reasons why the GM may support someone else for promotion. But the one reason you don't ever want is that the GM didn't know you wanted it, that you weren't hungry enough. Make sure you speak directly to what you want and then back it up with high performance.

ASK FOR MORE RESPONSIBILITY

No, you haven't lost your mind. You're asking for more responsibility, not more work; there's a big difference. Ask for projects that will provide you with more experience, more knowledge, and more skills to help your credibility but more importantly, to separate you from the other assistants. How many other assistants have asked for more responsibility? If you answered zero, you'd be right.

NEVER ASK FOR COMPLIMENTS OR UNNECESSARY ADVICE

Asking for compliments makes you seem needy because you are being needy.

Asking for unnecessary advice will make you seem like you are sucking up, because you are sucking up and your GM will absolutely and positively know it.

DO NOT GET THE 'DISEASE TO PLEASE'

Be careful with this. Some new managers have an almost overwhelming need to please. These managers compliment the GM and employees for even the smallest things, but worse, avoid criticizing employees because it makes them "uncomfortable". If this is you, fight it. Most people recognize insincerity, and your employees know which managers are reluctant to criticize them. This "disease to please" kills your credibility. How does anyone know when you are sincere? Address employees who need criticizing and avoid needless and superficial flattery.

DON'T TAKE CRITICISM PERSONALLY

Eventually, you're going to be criticized by the GM. No matter how great you have been, you're going to screw up and everyone hates criticism.

It is difficult to not take criticism personally, but the screw up is about work, not you. Some new managers make the mistake by responding to criticism by being aggressive and argumentative or by being sullen and withdrawn.

If you have those kinds of reactions, your GM may become reluctant to give you criticism because they just don't want the hassle that telling you brings. So, guess what? You don't get the feedback that you need to grow, learn, and improve.

HOW TO HANDLE CRITICISM

Listen carefully and then say back what the GM said. When you repeat it back, you've given your GM credit for the feedback and second, it will hurt less once you've repeated it back. As a past GM, I was always impressed when an assistant manager did not get defensive and was open to criticisms. If the GM gives you suggestions about how to get better, great. But often it is up to you to make a plan to get better.

WHAT IF THE CRITICISM IS NOT JUSTIFIED?

It is best to still acknowledge the GM's perception ("I can see how you would think that"). Then come up with a game plan to change the perception.

MENTOR

Some think that mentors just appear. They'll notice you, tap you on the shoulder, and say, "I'd like to be your mentor".

That's probably not going to happen.

You're the one who must initiate. Don't wait to be invited to be a mentee, since it could be, like, forever. Keep your eyes open for potential mentors. You might join industry associations or might notice someone in another part of the company. Regardless, you're the one who has to initiate.

Try to recognize when colleagues (or others) are interested in becoming mentors, even when they are not direct about it. It might happen like this: A senior manager asks about the kinds of challenges you are facing. Most people might just think the older manager is being nice. But you just might see potential and strike up a relationship.

Once you have a mentor, you've got to put in a lot of work to make sure that it gets off the ground. Keep in frequent contact with your mentor to keep the relationship strong.

Always come prepared to any meeting. If you have a problem that you want to share with your mentor, make sure you have a few solutions that you want the mentor to review and offer advice.

Be personable and have a positive attitude.

READY

You are promotable when your GM sees you as being able to handle GM.

When the GM sees you as a peer.

Talks to you about problems.

When the GM perceives you as ready for the next step.

Be the best damn manager when you're at work

DEVELOPMENT OF AN
ASSISTANT MANAGER

from 'There's a Hole in My Sidewalk', by Portia Nelson

I

I walk down the street
There is a deep hole in the sidewalk.
I fall in.
I am lost. I am helpless.
It isn't my fault.
It takes forever to find a way out.

II

I walk down the same street.
There is a deep hole in the sidewalk.
I fall in again.
I can't believe I'm in the same place, but it isn't my fault.
It still takes a long time to get out.

III

I walk down the same street.
There is a deep hole in the sidewalk.
I see it there.
I still fall in. It is a habit.
My eyes are open.
I know where I am.
It is my fault.
I get out immediately.

IV

I walk down the same street.
There is a deep hole in the sidewalk.
I walk around it.

V

I walk down a different street.

CHAPTER 18

REALITY CHECK

What's really happening

THERE'S A QUIZ, TEST, AND FINAL EVERY DAY

Most people think when they finish school, they've seen the last of tests, grades, pop quizzes, and final exams. Unfortunately, that is not true. Each contact you have with your GM is a pop quiz. Every question asked of you is a test, and every time you go to work, you're graded.

In school, a student could bring up his/her grade point average the next semester by studying more or simply dropping a course that was failing.

In management, it doesn't work that way. Your grade is cumulative. "C's" won't get you promoted; you need all "A's". In business, "F" stands for fired. There are no make-ups, no starting a new semester, and no do-overs. Your GM remembers all your grades and your reputation gets stronger or weaker every day.

Promotable managers continuously keep track of their reputations so that if it ever get off track, they know the problem and fix it before it can damage their reputations so badly that it cannot be repaired.

Obviously, it is far better to know as soon as possible if you are going in the wrong direction. It is always easier to change direction when caught early enough that the GM's negative perception is only temporary.

OUR JOBS, OUR CAREERS

Many of us are defined by our jobs. Careers become the most important part of our lives, with families and friends often feeling ignored. After all, we spend so much time at work, we like the people we work with, we like the work itself, and we enjoy the challenges of each day. It is no wonder that we throw ourselves into our jobs and have such a tremendous influence on our lives. When our jobs go well, we feel good about ourselves, our personal life, and our entire outlook tends to be positive.

However, what happens when we're no longer valued at work? How would you feel if you knew that the GM had labeled you as mediocre or worse? When our jobs go negative, they can cause serious effects that reach even further than the job. We feel insecure, our self-worth goes down, and invariably affects our personal life leaving us to feel powerless.

BEST TO KNOW

In some cases, you might think the GM likes you and thinks you are doing a good job because the GM occasionally asks about your car, family, or favorite sports team. But this might not be so. This same GM might just slam you during your formal performance review. Bottom line? Best to know, not guess, how your GM perceives you.

Barbara is a very personable and outgoing woman in her early twenties. She had been a server with a small restaurant chain for about a year when the company started to expand. She heard of an opening for an administrative assistant position to the GM that could lead to making the leap into management.

Barbara thought that this was an excellent opportunity to grow with the company. After all, she had been an employee for a long time and the move seemed perfect. She was excited when she got the job.

Time went quickly and she was pleased with her growing responsibilities. In fact, besides her normal duties, the GM had started giving her responsibilities that included many tasks that were typical of a manager. She was proud of the fact that the GM seemed to rely on her. She was confident in her ability and was excited to a part of this rapidly expanding company.

She had been administrative assistant for about a year when an incident happened that opened her eyes to reality. One of her duties was to get a report from all the assistant managers at the beginning of each week. She always had trouble with one particular assistant manager who was continually late. When she reminded him, he would usually say something derogatory to her.

One morning, it happened again, but today, she was tired of it. She called her GM to tell him the problem. The GM listened to her describe the behavior of the assistant manager, but instead of being sympathetic and counseling the assistant manager for continually hassling her, he said, "You're just having trouble because you're young and female".

She was indignant and bitter. She was also in shock. She had always thought that she was moving ahead. She had thought the GM was grooming her to become a manager. She had certainly thought the GM considered her as capable, mature, and able to get along with the employees and managers in the restaurant.

It was a startling realization for her that in her GM's eyes, she was just young and female. She realized then that she was not going to be promoted. She was determined to not waste another minute trying to make the GM change the way he saw her. She decided at that moment to change jobs. Once her decision was made, she felt calm because she now had a plan. Within two weeks, she had a management position in an environment where she could grow.

HINDSIGHT

There were indicators all along that this chauvinistic attitude was present. Barbara thought back to many times that she had been talked down to by the GM. He would say little things that were derogatory about her age, yet right after he said it, he would say that he could see her as an assistant manager. She had focused on the carrot of promotion and had been blinded that she could overcome age and gender discrimination by working hard and keeping a professional attitude.

Thinking back, she started putting together the other signs that had been there, but she had just shrugged off. One big one she missed was that there were no women in management.

Any part of the above may not have been significant by themselves. However, taken collectively, they meant that Barbara had faced an impossible challenge.

Your GM's perception of you is the key to your survival and your

---

The sooner you know how you are doing, the sooner you can either *stop* doing what you should *not* be doing or *start* doing what you *should* be doing.

Ideally, the GM monitors your progress, reviews your performance, and then makes suggestions in a regular and timely manner. When you have frequent feedback, even if you do screw up, only minor corrections will be necessary to get back on track and shouldn't cause any real damage to your credibility as a manager.

Unfortunately, assistant managers do not always receive open, timely, and relevant feedback. With no feedback, the potential for assistant managers to feel overconfident is strong yet might not be reality. All may not be well. The wise assistant manager seeks out and is aware of clues in any way possible.

IMMEDIATE FEEDBACK

Let's start with how not to do it. Don't wait until your regular performance review since you'll wait a month or up to 6 months to find out that you have been screwing up the entire time! No, you want and need much more immediate feedback.

1. Make it clear to your GM that you want and value the GM's insight on your performance, especially when you do something new or how you might improve on the next task.

2. No need for a formal meeting. Just pull your GM aside after a shift and ask for feedback to the shift or any specific situation that you're not sure you handled correctly. The GM should not mind at all. In fact, most GMs appreciate that you are trying to learn from them.

WARNING Don't ask for feedback just to suck up to the GM. Don't ask for feedback for situations when you know you've done a good job, or your question has an obvious answer. Only ask for feedback when you have a situation where you really want to learn; otherwise, your GM will see you as a suck-up killing any impression that you're really serious about becoming a better manager.

3. Have brief meetings every 2 weeks with your GM to discuss how you did the previous 2 weeks. Lengthen this to once a month if the meetings go well. This is just a casual check-in with your GM. Checking in weekly might be too soon to see any results and too much of a pain for the GM. Monthly meetings could be too long if you're doing something wrong. Of course, if the GM wants it at longer or shorter intervals, so be it.

4. Make sure you make it clear that you want just a very short meeting and that you want real feedback, especially negative feedback. That way, if you're way off, then you've only been way off for two weeks, and it will be relatively easy to stop what you're doing and start what you should be doing. This will go a long way in getting the GM to see you as committed to doing a superior job and serious about your career.

FEEDBACK

Receiving feedback can be stressful because well, you're being criticized. But trust me on this, you want to know sooner rather than later if the GM has criticisms.

Ignoring or avoiding criticism is career suicide

You want to know so that you can do something about it. Early criticisms avoid negative perceptions from forming with the GM.

- Ask for feedback in real time. Don't wait till the next shift or next week.

- Ask specific questions to get helpful information and examples.

- Feedback can be brief, informal coaching moments during or after shifts, in the walk-in, or just about anywhere.

Know how you are perceived by the GM so
you can do something about it.
Not knowing means you're just pulling shifts

BLINDED

Some assistants find themselves in positions where they were great only to find their status has gone down. The reasons are varied: a new GM comes in and immediately doesn't like them. Some may have been hurt by some past incident that caused their GM to view them negatively. Whatever reason, the result is a realization that your GM does not think of you as promotable. You realize that you must do something, perhaps a drastic something, to change that perception.

It takes time and energy to build a career and it takes even more time and energy to turn around a negative perception. One obstacle is that most people view their own performance as excellent; it must be their GM's perception that is wrong.

This type of thinking, even though it might make you feel better, does not help the situation and, in fact, usually causes greater harm.

It's not enough to simply be good at what you do.
If your GM perceives you poorly, you won't be successful.

GIVING OFF THE WRONG IMAGE

You heard that another assistant thinks you're "bossy". You're surprised. You never thought of yourself that way, in fact, you thought of yourself as the opposite, because you have trouble telling people to do something.

Finding that others see you differently from the way you see yourself can be troubling. Small differences are no big deal, but big ones should be taken seriously. Recognizing big differences in perception helps you become effective in your career and social relationships.

The more you feel the need to see yourself in a certain way, the more your perceptions can be tied to wishful thinking and denial.

FIRST STEP

The first step is to find out the truth of the perception. Are you sure it's negative? Why is the perception negative? What caused it? How severe is it? What can be done about it? Being proactive about your career is the most beneficial behavior that you can do for yourself.

SOMETHING HAS CHANGED

You're rolling along in your career. You have a good rapport with your GM who always asks about your family or hobbies or what you did on your off day. Then one day the GM doesn't. Something is up. And not in a good way.

Some GMs are conflict adverse, so when their perception of you changes, they become passive aggressive or give off only nonverbal clues, instead of going to you directly.

Be aware of telltale signs. No more small talk, feeling that the GM is avoiding you, other changes in the way you're treated could be indications that your GM just may have a problem with your performance.

If you suspect something is wrong, don't wait for a formal performance review. Get a meeting with the GM to fix any problem before it is too late to fix. But, just to be safe, it can't hurt to take a look at your resume and make sure it's up to date.

In the first book, I laid out the right way to approach the GM for this very important meeting.

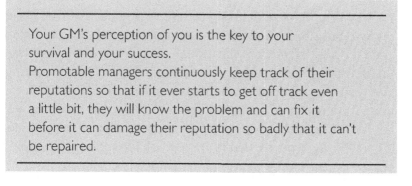

Your GM's perception of you is the key to your survival and your success.
Promotable managers continuously keep track of their reputations so that if it ever starts to get off track even a little bit, they will know the problem and can fix it before it can damage their reputation so badly that it can't be repaired.

EXPECTATIONS

The GM plays such a critical part in the success of every new manager that great pains must be taken to understand the GM's expectations. You've got to continuously pay attention if you are meeting those expectations by being aware of signals that the GM gives out regarding your performance.

- Make it clear to your GM that you want and value the GM's insight on your performance. You want the GM's views on how you could improve especially when you did something new, or you've faced an unusual situation.

- Just pull your GM aside after a shift and request a reaction to the shift or feedback on any

DENIAL

Denial can come from two different sources. If you're just starting out, you just might not recognize early warning signs that your job might be in danger. If you've just been hanging on, you may be reluctant to risk what little you have. Either way, denial can cost you time, possibly missing an opportunity to fix whatever was wrong.

UH OH – YOUR REVIEW WENT BAD

It's normal to feel defensive or angry (or both!) during a bad review. But don't. Stay calm, stay professional. Simply listen and take notes; Don't act on emotion. At the end of the meeting, thank the GM for the feedback. Spend a day or two examining how you feel, then set up another meeting with the GM for a more in-depth examination of the review. In this meeting, ask for specific examples of your poor performance. For example, if the GM says you are disorganized, ask for concrete examples of how your disorganization hurt your work.

Asking for specifics helps you understand what you did wrong and makes it more difficult for the GM to make general, subjective statements without evidence.

Sometimes, it is possible to fix the situation and go on to flourish in the job. Other times, a bad review indicates it is time to update your resume.

Tell the GM that you will come up with a plan to improve your performance. You must do this yourself. Do not ask the GM for assistance in your plan. This is your career, and you need to take responsibility for it, not the GM. Once you've got the plan, set up a follow up meeting.

Then schedule regular meetings with the GM throughout the year to discuss your progress toward the goals you set in the plan. Good managers tend to give their employees continuing feedback anyway but always initiate those discussions and have them built into the plan.

A BAD REVIEW CAN BE A WAKEUP CALL

Sometimes a bad review can be a super good thing. It can force you to really look at the job you have and question if it is really the job you want to have.

I gave a bad review to an assistant who actually hated being in the front of the house and hated being around customers. He was a terrific guy but was just not suited to being a restaurant manager since dealing with customers is kind of a big deal. After his review, he realized that he could never make GM and that the reason was that he was not suited for the restaurant business. It was amazing to see how this realization made him excited to start a new path. He thanked me for being direct and honest. A bad review can give a reality check that can save assistants months or even years in a job that was doomed to never lead to advancement, much less a job to enjoy.

WHAT DID ANNA DO?

Anna was an excellent assistant manager in a large restaurant chain. She enjoyed a great relationship with her GM who almost treated her as co-GM. She gave work 100 percent, often sacrificing time with her family. Everyone assumed that Anna was going to be the next general manager promoted.

Unknown to Anna, the GM was not well liked with his supervisor, who was over 5 restaurants, including the GM's. One day, the supervisor came in to tell all the assistants that the GM had been terminated and introduced the new GM.

It didn't take Anna long to realize that her career was in jeopardy. The new GM basically ignored her. At meetings, the new GM didn't make eye contact with her, and Anna found out that she was not going to meetings that other assistants were going to.

It was hard for Anna to be basically invisible, reduced to a minor role, when before, she had been so vital to the restaurant and GM before. Anna guessed that the new GM did not like her because she had been so closely linked to the previous GM. She felt it was completely unfair that the new GM had not talked with her or given her a chance.

Anna became passive and quiet, the opposite of her usual outgoing personality. She put her job on autopilot, never taking initiative, and not reprimanding employees who, in the past, she would have given feedback. Anna's performance had dropped to below even an average assistant manager. She just could not get motivated. Anna was falling into a vicious cycle in which negative perception leads to questioning her value, leading to decreased performance, making the new GM think he was right to have a negative perception.

Anna had to make a choice: quit or change the GM's perception.

WHAT ANNA DID:

After agonizing over her decision, Anna chose to fight the negative perception. After all, she was proud of the company, and she believed she could be a success. As a new manager with a significant other with a good job, she wasn't excited about the possibility of relocating. Plus, she didn't want to just walk away from a job where she had worked so hard and sacrificed her family so much. After all that, she did not want to find a new job and reestablish herself all over again. She was good at what she did, and that had not changed.

She believed she could overcome her new manager's perception and prove that she was valuable to the company. Anna also knew that her performance so far was hurting her reputation and reinforcing the new GM's negative perception of her.

Anna needed a turnaround strategy. This strategy is detailed in the previous book.

FLIGHT OR FIGHT?

Anna's decision was not unusual. When there is a crisis at work, most people would rather stay at their job rather than leave even when quitting would seem to be the way to go. Staying and changing the GM's negative perception requires an incredible amount of work.

Yet, most people stay for some reason:

- Their significant other has a great job
- Do not want to relocate
- Have relatives in the area
- Like the schools that their kids go
- Almost vested in a financial plan
- Love the job
- Love the people they work with
- Don't want to prove themselves again

You absolutely cannot believe that you are the victim. The truth is that everything is within your control. Take action. Just ask Anna.

CHAPTER 19

IT'S ABOUT TIME

Managing yourself, friends, family, and work

Nowhere is time more crushing than in the restaurant business. Time management involves putting your available time to the best possible use. This is simple in concept but can be difficult to do.

Time management is not really about managing time, but about managing yourself. The keys are planning and priority setting. As a restaurant manager, you'll always have hundreds of things to do, but to manage time effectively, you've got to stay focused on what's important because it is incredibly easy to get sidetracked by any one of hundreds of unexpected events in a shift.

WATCH OUT FOR TIME BANDITS AND TIME LEAKS

Unproductive habits and problematic employees rob time from you during the day until the day is gone and you have nothing to show for it except getting through the shift. You've done nothing to move your career forward. Surviving the shift is not enough.

During shifts, many new managers find themselves changing toilet paper rolls or sweeping the front. Can no one else do these? This is when delegating can save a lot of time.

Then there are the negative employees. All employees (and managers) have problems, but negative employees think their problems should be everyone's problems. Left alone, these negative employees can drive away customers, disrupt morale, and completely rob management of time and energy faster than a sewer backup.

INSUFFICIENT PLANNING

When you're running the shift, you are in charge of a multimillion-dollar business. You've got to have a daily action plan to keep you focused and show your progress for the shift. Spending just 15 minutes at the start of your shift can be the difference between a productive shift and just getting through the shift.

"Other people make too many demands on my time"

Others should not control how *you* spend your time, you should control how you spend your time. If other people have that much control over your time, you are letting them control you. One of your most effective time savers can be learning to say no. When saying no, be courteous, give a *short* explanation of why you can't, and avoid lengthy discussions about your reasons.

Obviously, all tasks and projects do not have the same importance. Managers often feel they must respond to situations or persons who are loudest or press the most. This causes managers to solve problems as they arrive, do the easy work first, or take care of the difficult work first on the assumption that is the fastest way to get rid of them.

Don't do that.

Deal with things in a logical, orderly sequence. If you deal with matters in the order they occur, it is usually unproductive. Important does not mean urgent, and urgent does not always mean important.

TAKE A LOOK

Everyone has the same amount of time. The question is are you using the time effectively? Are you doing things that are unnecessary? Are you doing things that only you can do? If you are, that's great. But if you're doing some things that can be delegated, delegate!

PLAN THE WORK AND WORK THE PLAN

You can make the most effective use of your time by planning and getting organized. The object is to be sure that you have enough time to meet your specific goals.

Make monthly goals, then break them down to weekly, and then daily to-do lists that you will absolutely, positively get done each day.

Evaluate your progress twice per day. Take a look at how you're doing about one third of the way through the shift and about two thirds of the way. Will you meet your objective for the shift? If not, what got in the way?

Being busy is not the same as being productive

WANT TO FEEL SUPERIOR? DON'T PROCRASTINATE

It is really, really easy to procrastinate. I mean who wants to do something you don't like to do or is trivial? As a new restaurant manager, I was one of the world's greatest procrastinators. But that all came to a screeching stop when I had put off finishing an employee schedule until the day before it was due. I couldn't believe when I was called in to cover a manager who got into an accident. I was forced to finish the schedule at the end of my shift at like 2am in the morning. That was it. Never again. I was done with procrastinating. Don't be me.

I'm convinced that waiting till the last-minute causes shifts in the universe that makes things happen to punish you for procrastinating. Like the power goes out when it has not gone out in 122 years. Or the printer runs out of ink. Or your pet decides that now would be a great time to escape.

You're screwed.

The good news about that is that it usually breaks someone of procrastinating ever again. Like it did me.

The problem is that each day you procrastinate, the task gets more serious. What was a mild issue on Monday, becomes urgent by Friday. We all know that procrastination hurts our careers, but still cannot seem to stop procrastinating.

It seems weird to mention procrastination now, because I haven't been that person for a very long time. One step that can help is to divide big tasks into little steps or tasks. Sometimes that helps move away from procrastination. It helped me.

BUT FOR THE THINGS YOU HATE TO DO OR CONSIDER TRIVIAL?

The one thing that helped me from procrastinating was the amazing smugness and sense of superiority that I felt when I was ahead of schedule and finished something ahead of my deadline. Think about how good you'll feel knowing you got this, rather than feeling pathetic and weak when you miss your deadline. Promotable managers do not miss deadlines, which means they don't procrastinate.

MAKE TIME FOR WHAT MATTERS

If you've got a goal to accomplish, stay focused, and get it done. Beware of time wasters. This does *not* mean to not take time to break the hundred for the bartender. It means to *not* get caught in the trap of wasting time with anything that is not essential. Anything that is about operations is essential. But when a server wants to talk about his car or wants your advice about his roommate, they can wait. When you allow yourself to go off on tangents, you'll think there is not enough time in the day to do anything. And guess what? You're right, nothing gets done. Focus on what your goal is for the shift.

DON'T DO THIS

Because you want to be perceived as a hard worker, you're OK if the GM sees you flying around the restaurant. You've got lots to do and you're getting it done!

Wrong. You may look energetic, but you may also come across as frantic and out of control. Your GM will think you can't handle more responsibility since you're just barely handling what you've got. This is the wrong approach.

You don't want to come across as frazzled. You want to be in control and calm. Put your preventive manager hat on and take off the "look at me. I'm putting out fires" hat.

IMBALANCE IS UNAVOIDABLE

You'd think that managing yourself might involve some kind of work life balance, and you'd be right. But realistically, achieving any kind of work life balance is extremely difficult when you are trying to establish your reputation in management.

Work-life balance is when a person equally prioritizes the demands of one's career and the demands of one's personal life.

Unfortunately, I think this is pure fiction and a theoretical concept only.

You may think that the industry or the company that you are in now has absolutely the worst work life balance in the entire country, maybe even in the entire known universe.

And you just might be right. But you're not alone. I don't know of any industry or company which doesn't expect promotable managers to work hard and work long. The two concepts; establishing your reputation in your career and spending equal time with your family, are completely incompatible.

"Come on oil, learn to love water! Mix it! You can do it!"

Unfortunately, just like oil and water, you can't.

Our desire to succeed professionally can push us to set aside our family in favor of work. There is only so much time in the day. The company wants a large piece, and your significant other deserves a large piece. Unfortunately, you don't have two large pieces available. You just can't do it.

Looking back on my career with my weak (pathetic) attempts to achieve some kind of work life balance, I now believe that it can't be done or at least can't be done well. At different times, either work or family will always take precedence over the other, but is especially true when just starting out, trying your best to get ahead.

What you can strive to do is to not allow one to always take precedence over the other. When you sense that one is truly taking hold for the long term, do what you can to bring it back as soon as possible.

BUT THERE IS HOPE

What can help is if you concentrate on working smart (not just hard) and keeping your significant other informed about what is happening at work. If he/she knows when you have a critical time/ project, it'll go a long way into understanding and cutting down friction.

Of course, the flip side means that when there is no critical time or project, that you put a priority on the family. But be careful, for it is really easy to slip back and start to stay late, make excuses, and once again start to neglect the family with the justification that you're working for the family. Don't. When you've finished your day, go home. Exit the closest door.

YOU'VE GOTTA TRY: THE GOOD STUFF

We all want work-life balance. We want it because it brings less stress, lowers risk of burnout, and gives a greater sense of well-being. Here are some ways to create a better work-life balance:

Accept that there is no perfect work-life balance.

When you have to sacrifice home over work, it's normal to feel guilty and frustrated. It is easy to blame your GM, your work, or karma when you do not have balance in your life. When this happens, it is even easier to feel that your work is not satisfying and start to look for irritations that used to be easily overlooked or unimportant before. This dissatisfaction can also cause you to be irritable at your significant other.

Either way, it isn't good for the home team. Something has to give.

One thought may help: Balance should be thought of as achieved over time, not each day

TAKE TIME OFF

So many of us resist taking vacations that we earned. New managers often worry that work will do better without them or that work will do worse without them. Whichever way it goes, each would make them look bad. But fight this and take the vacation. You've earned it. Enjoy it. You'll come back even better.

MAKE TIME FOR YOURSELF AND YOUR FAMILY

It may seem weird to schedule one-on-one time with someone you live with, but it can ensure that you spend quality time with them.

KEEP ON LEARNING: BEING A BETTER YOU

Have you had 3 years of experience?

or

1 year of experience 3 times?

There's a big difference.

DIVERSITY AND ADVERSITY BEAT REPETITION

Push yourself to go after difficult jobs. The best learning happens the more outside your comfort zone you get. When you tackle more difficult jobs, experience personnel problems, have severe profit pressure, or have difficult employees, you'll learn. Painful yes, but you'll grow.

Even though these all sound like they suck (and they do), you'll learn the most. You just can't stay in your comfort zone to get better. You're trying to get yourself ready for taking on larger roles and responsibilities. Get the experience now while you have support, not when you're the GM and expected to know a lot more.

REFLECT – WHAT REALLY HAPPENED? WHY DID IT HAPPEN?

It's tough to question yourself. But it is a really useful tool that you can train yourself to do. When a situation did not go well, ask yourself: What really happened? Why did it happen? Could I have handled it differently? What did I learn? Discuss with your GM to get more insight.

GET FEEDBACK

It is really tough to be objective about yourself. And it may be even tougher to ask for raw, objective feedback when that feedback could be negative.

The best kind of feedback is when you're forced to think about what your assumptions were, why you thought a particular decision was the best one, and what alternatives could have been better. Ideally, your GM can help with this. Ask.

THE V WORD

One great way to broaden your experience is to volunteer (yes, the V word) for assignments, committees, initiatives, or focus groups when they come up. This is a great way to meet fellow managers and upper management in different parts of the company. You'll develop new skills, grow your network, and broaden your network by meeting a different set of managers. All of which just might help you later. Keep your eyes open for opportunities.

YOUR OWN DEVELOPMENT

Joining professional associations is a great way to develop professionally, broaden your network, and find out more about what is happening in your industry. Ask your GM which professional associations might be a good fit for you. Be careful, they can also be a potential time sink, so choose only those that are valued by your industry and will not interfere with work or family.

COMMIT TO DEVELOPING

Managers who constantly push themselves to grow and develop perform better and gets you noticed as promotable. They also differentiate themselves from other managers by constantly trying to get better.

To get started, add learning to your goals. Make a commitment to learn something new each quarter. There are many resources available such as LinkedIn Learning courses, online certifications, leadership seminars, books, and videos. Your GM just may pick up the tab too. Ask.

CRISIS MANAGEMENT

Fighting fires is distracting, time consuming and costly. If you find yourself in a cycle with one crisis following another, you're not planning enough. Make note of what caused the crisis. By reducing these experiences, you will become much more effective and less stressed.

Think back on the last crisis you faced and answer these questions:

Was the crisis new?

Was there anything predictable about the situation? Could you see it coming?

Is there anything you can do to prevent another similar situation occurring?

Often what seemed a crisis can be prevented by checklists or a little more planning, or maybe even developing a new procedure. Encourage your employees to bring up potential problems as early as possible to you.

No amount of planning can eliminate all crises, but planning can reduce those that are repetitive or predictable. By reducing the crises, you'll have more time and smoother shifts.

If it wasn't for the last minute; nothing would get done

CHAPTER 20

EVERY SHIFT IS YOUR CAREER

If you're the boss and you stop rowing, don't be surprised if everyone else stops rowing

I f you're reading this book, you obviously care about your career. One important part in your career is how and what you do each day. What you do (or don't do) during your shifts are super important.

Many managers think of shifts as something to get through. But when you think about it, **what you do each shift adds up to your career.** That's why it is so important to use each shift to move your career forward rather than just be a series of days that might (or might not) get you promoted.

Many managers tend to put their energy into the busiest part of the shift because that's when they feel a sense of urgency but then relax when the rush is over. This is understandable, but they're wasting a great opportunity to get a lot done that would get them out earlier in the short term and advance their career in the long term.

Go into each shift like it is the most important shift you'll ever work. Imagine the CEO is visiting and wants to shadow you. Smile, visit customers, genuinely care about your employees and guests.

Your goal is to be the best assistant manager in the company. The energy and attitude that you bring to each shift will be the exact same energy and attitude that your employees show their customers. You have an incredible amount of influence, both positive and negative, and it is up to you which one your employees feel.

Say hello to every employee when you first come into the restaurant. Genuinely listen to your employees and get to know them. Be in a good mood, be passionate about your job and let that good mood be contagious to the employees and to the guests. Have that one thing that you're going to accomplish this shift and get it done.

You are already in charge; you don't need to prove it. The higher up in management you get, usually the more humble you become and the more you listen. Remember, you have the final say, so it can't hurt to get other opinions. Your employees will appreciate you asking their opinions and helps build your reputation.

Have personal one on ones with your employees every day. These are casual, but you'll get to know your employees in a very short period of time. "How's work going for you?" "Can you think of anything that might improve things?"

Don't be afraid of difficult conversations but do approach issues in a meaningful and effective way. Focus on the behavior, not the person.

Be early. Always.

Appreciate your employees. Treat them with respect. Support them and lead them.

It is your job to develop your employees.

Say thank you, like a million times.

Everyone in the restaurant is equal. You treat busboys, line cooks, dishwashers, everyone with the same respect.

At the end of the day, taking care of guests and running a good shift are priorities.

ON "BEING RIGHT"

It is important to not worry so much about being "right". When there is a customer complaint, genuinely apologize to the guest. Never apologize with the slightest patronizing, condescending or irritated tone. If you cannot be genuine with your apology, regardless of whether you are right or wrong, you're wrong.

IMPORTANT! When you (the new guy) are ready to make changes to a procedure (or anything), let your employees know why you're making changes. If you don't, they'll assume you're making changes to make things easier for you, rather than a better way.

CONSIDER THIS:

Good and bad managers, effective and lazy managers, all work about the same number of hours. So, if you're going to be at work anyway, make the most of it. I guarantee that you will be promoted much sooner than the manager who only puts in the minimum effort. The benefits to you include smooth shifts, employee respect, and a career that takes care of itself.

YOUR EMPLOYEES KNOW

Trust me on this: your employees know which employees get out of work. They also know which managers can be manipulated by complaining. The bottom line is good employees resent lazy employees, but they resent "weak" managers even more. It will be a hassle at first, but force yourself to ask difficult employees to do things you normally would only ask your favorites to do.

The "bad" employees will resist the new you. They'll think you turned on them and are unfair. But you will be doing the entire restaurant a great service by making it run more efficiently and fairly and you have greatly strengthened your management skills. Morale will go up and I guarantee that you will be a far better manager.

HARD OR SOFT SHOULD BE HARD AND SOFT

Many new managers are confused as to whether they should be "hard" or "soft" with their employees. This is a great question that comes up with every new manager.

And the answer is yes.

You should and need to be able to be both. Think of hard and soft as tools in your toolbox. If you only had "hard" tools, what would you do when you needed a soft tool? And vice versa. You need to be able to use both. The real challenge is force yourself to go against your natural tendencies to be one or the other. This is tough, and unfortunately, sometimes you have to get burned to find out that the key is to use hard when it is needed and use soft when it is needed. If you use hard when soft would have been better or vice versa, bad things happen. Sometimes only through experience will you figure this out.

YOU ARE NOT INDISPENSABLE

Everyone is replaceable at work, even you. No matter how important you think you are, you're not. After I had opened a new concept as GM for a chain, I started to feel indispensable when I got transferred. How could the restaurant possibly do

well with me not there since I was the reason it was so successful? I just knew it would totally fall apart when I left. Well,
after I got transferred, the restaurant did even better, thank
you very much.

Be confident, not cocky.

THE CARE AND FEEDING OF YOUR GM

E veryone sees the need to manage their employees, but some have a problem with the concept
of managing their GM. But wait, it makes sense.

Effective assistant managers not only manage down with
their employees, but also manage sideways with their peers,
and upwards with their GMs. This is *not* about trying to manip-
ulate or suck up to your GM. This is about trying to build a
relationship with your GM that involves mutual respect and
understanding. This allows you to avoid many (many!) potential
problems down the road.

UNDERSTANDING YOUR GM

At a minimum, appreciate your GM's goals, pressures,
strengths, and weaknesses. Do you know how the GM prefers
you to check in and how often? Does the GM prefer to micromanage by requiring frequent detailed explanations before you
do anything or does the GM take more of a hands-off approach
allowing you to be independent with only occasional meetings?

If your GM is a micromanager, the GM will micromanage,
you're not going to change that. But you can head this off by
giving frequent updates which usually satisfies this type of GM.
If your GM is more hands-off, frequent check-ins would irritate
and cause this GM to think you are insecure. It is important for
you to know and adapt to the GM, not the other way around,
which is a small price to pay to have a great relationship.

UNDERSTAND YOURSELF

Thankfully, you have control here. Are you naturally argumentative or are you naturally non-confrontational? Does either style drive the GM nuts? You are not going to change your personality or have any luck in changing your GM's. But you *can* be aware of your personality style and adapt to the GMs to make your relationship with the GM much more effective and natural.

MUTUAL EXPECTATIONS

Don't assume you know what the GM expects from you. Some GMs spell out their expectations. That's great, but many don't. You cannot assume that you know the GM's expectations and the burden to find out falls on you. I suggest writing down all the expectations that you *think* you know (budget cost percentages, turnover, hiring and training expectations, cleanliness, etc.), then having a quick meeting to go over them with the GM to see if they are in line with the GM. Most GM's will appreciate that you have taken the initiative to be sure, rather than guess.

USE THE GM'S TIME WISELY

If you think you never have enough time, your GM feels exactly the same. Every time you ask a question, you have used up some time from both of you. Before you rush over to ask a question to the GM, think about what you have to ask. Each GM is different: Some welcome questions, but some will bite your head off it is trivial or if you could have answered the question yourself.

YOUR GM LOOKS GOOD, YOU LOOK GOOD

It is important to pay attention to opportunities that come along when your GM could use some help. This is not playing up to the boss, it is simply helping your career. It is a pure win-win situation, since when the GM looks good, the team looks good, and the people who helped, will get the most help back. I have never seen a GM forget when an assistant manager put in extra effort to help them. It may not help you immediately, but you are planting seeds that could do you invaluable good one day and mean another step closer to promotion.

After helping or at least *offering* to help, you just might notice a difference in your relationship with the GM. The GM may feel that she has an ally in you. You might notice the GM asking your opinions more. That one helpful incident may get the GM to start thinking of you as promotable.

MANAGE YOUR GM BY THINKING LIKE A GM

Thinking like a GM takes thinking much more objectively and minimizing emotion. It has been my experience that most, if not all job promotions happen when least expected. All of us have cycles in our jobs, kind of like mood swings, that cause our performance to go up and down. It's easy to get lulled into this up and down rhythm because events happen that can cause us to lose focus and consequently lower our performance. Real pressures at home, such as illness, divorce, money problems or home repairs can cause these lapses.

But more commonly, it is caused by getting too comfortable, just relaxing a bit, and putting work on autopilot. Anytime performance falls, even slightly, it gets noticed. Unfortunately, this is exactly when opportunities for promotions come up; when you're at the low point or on the downward curve. This slight dip causes doubts in your GM and places you out of promotion.

Promotable managers maintain a consistently high level of job performance by smoothing out the normal peaks and valleys.

'GOOD ENOUGH ISN'T!'

The difference between mediocre work and excellent work can be only a few percentage points. If you can consistently condition yourself to do excellent work and not just OK work, you are well on your way to becoming promotable.

NO BUT'S!

But I'm on time everyday

But I stay late and come in early

But I've never called in sick

But I'm a team player and get along with everyone

None of that matters as much as you might think they do because those are all minimums that are expected, not extras. Those buts are used by assistant managers who didn't meet budget or some other responsibility and expect those to help somehow.

They won't.

PART SIX

YOUR PROMOTION JOURNEY

CHAPTER 22

SETTING YOURSELF UP FOR SUCCESS

If you don't know where you're going, you're going to end up somewhere else

Laurence J. Peter, The Peter Principle

One common mistake that new restaurant managers make is to bust their butts everyday but never take time to think about their career. Many managers assume their company has a plan, and they might, but you should never just sit around waiting for the plan to happen and assume the plan *will* happen. No, you have a personal career plan that includes milestones and a timetable.

I made this mistake. Without a plan, I was tempted to take opportunities that were not what I had planned for myself, but I was so flattered that I sometimes took them. Looking back, I took these (wrong) opportunities because I did not have a career plan to guide me and prevent those kinds of detours. These detours wasted a lot of my time before I realized that I had gone away from what I really wanted. Save yourself detours that can cause you much grief and time by sticking to your career plan.

THE START OF YOUR CAREER

Your career in restaurant management usually starts as manager trainee, advances to assistant manager, then on to general manager and beyond. The first phase of your career (manager trainee and assistant manager) is mostly technical (learning how to do the jobs of employees who report to you) and the many functions of managers (budgets, problem solving, customer relations, scheduling, managing shifts, ordering, making deposits, and hundreds of others).

This book concentrates on your journey to your first major promotion, that of general manager. I have always thought this promotion from assistant manager to GM is the most difficult promotion for assistant managers because, for a very large part, assistants are almost totally dependent on their GMs for their advancement.

General managers, by comparison, have the advantage that their performance is judged by the performance of the restaurant without relying on a middleman (the GM in the assistant manager's case) for advancement.

BEWARE UNREALISTIC EXPECTATIONS

When companies see management applications that have three or four jobs on it all as assistant manager, never at the GM level, companies think that the applicant must have either unrealistic expectations and is too impatient to stay until making the next level or a lack of talent, people skills, or something else too difficult to overcome. Either way, they're not going to consider hiring because the applicant is too much of a risk. Bottom line: Choose your company wisely and try to hang in there till you reach GM.

HOW DO YOU SET YOURSELF UP FOR SUCCESS?

You want a personally satisfying career. To do this, you're going to have to be prepared to take charge of your career and become a self-directed learner. You're going to have to occasionally pursue or create developmental opportunities, experiences, and relationships to learn.

In starting your career, you need a great deal of technical learning (how to wait tables, schedule, bartend), conceptual (strategy), and human relations (how to manage and motivate). But to be effectively on the fast track, you must be prepared to learn about yourself, make necessary changes, and cope with stress and emotions. Self-knowledge and emotional maturity have been found to be a key characteristic of effective managers.

There was a study conducted years ago with a kindergarten class. The students were told each would be given a cookie and then the teacher would leave the room. If the cookie was not eaten by the time the teacher returned, they would be given two more cookies. The researchers were hidden and watched while the teacher was gone. Some immediately ate the cookie; some walked around trying to not look at the cookie, but ate it eventually, some just did some other activity to take their mind off of the cookie.

The researchers tracked the students for twenty-five years. They found that the students who were able to wait for the teacher to return did much better professionally than the students who gave in to instant gratification and ate their cookie.

Putting off eating a cookie now, rather than the promise of more cookies later was tough for 5-year-olds. But it can still be difficult for adult managers. Thinking long term is worth it because your career is worth it.

One great exercise is to take a personality test called the Enneagram. There are literally hundreds of articles, websites, and books written about it. I think it is terrific to get to know your strengths and weaknesses. Another great resource are articles on EQ or Emotional Quotient.

AWARENESS

I hate to admit it, but when I first started in restaurant management, I don't think I had any awareness of what was going on. I just assumed the company would train me and then eventually promote me when I was ready.

I was never really aware of the length or quality of the training or whether I was ready to go to the next level. I was not proactive; I just waited for management.

When you are an assistant manager, know what you need in your progression to GM; keep track of your progress and know your expectations. Review your management progress with your GM on a regular basis and make sure that you stay on track. Good management and good companies should be able to go over how you are progressing. Don't be passive and stand on the sidelines. If you still don't understand how to do inventory, ask to do it. If you haven't been over the bar, ask to be over the bar. The squeaky wheel really does get the grease.

DEVELOPING YOURSELF

There is no short-cut for experience; "doing" is essential. But taking the time to develop yourself can accelerate this process. Observe your GM as the GM motivates, criticizes, and communicates: Make mental notes of what works and what doesn't work.

The dreaded V word: Volunteer

Ask for 'stretch' assignments or projects that are a little over your head. Just make sure you have the drive and persistence to do the job well.

KNOW YOUR STRENGTHS, BUT MORE IMPORTANTLY YOUR WEAKNESSES

It is great that you know that you suck at something. Great job! But that's not enough. To be on top of your game, you must take the next step and *do* something about it. This takes work on your part, but it is worth it. Start today.

Aligning your team: Communicate your directions in a clear and easy way. You must have credibility, empathy, and the ability to communicate with diverse employees and be willing to empower select employees thru delegation.

Motivate and inspire your people: As your credibility grows with your employees, your power grows. As your power grows, your influence grows. You will have the ability to change the behavior, attitudes, and values of your employees, regardless of how diverse they are. Your ability to coach and manage performance by providing feedback and rewards will grow at the same time.

Establish direction: You've got to be able to turn complex and often ambiguous information into straightforward, easily communicated directions for your team. This requires you to think about what you're going to say and able to answer questions. Make sure you think about what questions could be asked, so you can get answers before you meet with your team.

Don't rely on management alone to guide you to promotion. Sometimes, you will have to take the lead to push for another assignment or to cross train. But to start, let's go through a few basics:

Delegate: It is easy to "just do it". At first, just get comfortable with delegation, soon you'll be ready to actually do it. Selfishly, it helps you to do more. You can work on several projects at the same time and accomplish an amazing amount. It also helps to develop staff and lets the GM see that you care about developing staff. Development of those under you gets more important as you advance in your career. Break down large projects into chunks and, if possible, delegate the smaller chunks. In the first book, I explained how to do this, so I won't repeat.

GET A MENTOR

This is tougher than it appears to be because mentees are often chosen by the mentors, not the other way around. But you can be on the lookout for a potential mentor. Just ask them. The worse that can happen is they say no.

Caution: Mentors will devote plenty of time for you as long as you perform extremely well. But as soon as you slack off even a little, they will not have any time for you. If you're serious about having a mentor, bring only your 'A' game.

PROJECT CONFIDENCE

You cannot be an effective leader if you are frantic, arrogant, or insecure. Slow down, be humble, and be positive.

FOCUS ON THE BIGGER PICTURE

Don't just get into the trap of fighting fires, reacting to situations that could have been prevented. I admit that it feels good to solve or fix a problem, but spend your time and energy preventing the situations in the first place by planning.

GIVE AND TAKE CONSTRUCTIVE CRITICISM

Do not avoid corrective feedback to your staff. If you do, it will kill your credibility. When you give corrective feedback, focus on the negative employee behavior, not the person. You're more than just a "nice guy", you're their boss. You're trying to make the restaurant better.

REFLECTION

One of the most powerful things you can do for yourself after every critical situation, is to ask yourself what really happened? Why did it happen? What could I have done differently? If you go through this process, you'll find that you will not make that mistake again or get yourself into a particular situation again.

DECISIONS:

One of the big decisions you'll have to make is when you're asked to transfer. First, of course, is to consult your significant other. But as for your career, don't just say yes, make sure it makes sense to you and your significant other. If it is a lateral move, I would say yes ONLY if there is significant growth potential with the move. If it is to the same sales, same everything, ask your supervisor the reasons that it is a positive step for your career. I never did and I got transferred a lot. Most of the time I felt taken advantage of.

How to take a compliment

Say thank you.

Don't downplay the compliment. You may think it makes you look good, but it doesn't. Accept it gracefully.

CHAPTER 23

YOUR OPTIONS: Q AND A FOR A GREAT FIT

Full-service or Fast Food (Quick Service)?

Some managers tend to look down on quick service. They only see themselves in a full-service restaurant. But not so fast. Don't be too quick to judge. It really depends on what you're looking for.

One single McDonald's does over two and a half million dollars. That's not nothing. In fact, it is quite something. Sometimes, Quick Service restaurants can offer a faster path to GM and a multi-unit management position than full-service restaurants. So, if climbing the corporate ranks is a priority, take a hard look at quick service. As a side note, many fast-food restaurants are franchises, not company units. No problem at all with that, just be aware.

DO I GO WITH A FRANCHISE OR COMPANY OWNED? DOES IT MATTER?

Franchises can be huge with hundreds of restaurants, or they can be as small as one unit. They can be well run, and they can be poorly run. Depending on the size of the franchise, they can have the same structure and operate just like a corporate owned chain. As a very general rule, corporate stores probably tend to be more formal, with more layers of management. Bottom line: I don't think it matters but ask a lot of questions regarding structure and growth plans.

FAMILY-OWNED/INDEPENDENT OR CHAIN?

I usually recommend that a new restaurant manager go with a restaurant chain rather than a family/independent as a first company. Two main reasons: The first is that in a chain, you will be given between 2 to 4 months as a manager trainee with no management responsibilities where you will have time to train in each position, learn admin, and work with management BEFORE you have any real responsibility for supervising employees or costs.

In many, maybe not all, independent restaurants, they often do not have the luxury of having you train for any length of time with no responsibilities. Often, you will take over a department (servers, bar, etc.) immediately because you were hired to fill a management need.

While getting right in may sound good, it is probably not for a new manager. When you have little experience, having immediate responsibilities can be overwhelming since you are expected to perform immediately. This is multiplied if the restaurant has any cost or labor problems, which can get very frustrating since you have just become a manager and probably don't know how to fix problems. But the reality is that if you cannot fix the problem in a short period of time (maybe 3 months), you just might quit or be invited to quit.

The second reason is the lack of opportunity for growth in a single unit restaurant. Where can you go? Unless one of the daughters or sons is a potential marriage partner, there is probably very little promotion potential.

BUT. The other side of this, of course, is that you just may have landed in a perfect opportunity for growth. If the owner wants to grow the concept, this could be a golden opportunity to be on the ground floor as the company expands.

MY OWN DISASTER WITH A FAMILY-OWNED RESTAURANT CHAIN

The story begins when I was totally happy as GM in a chain with rumors that I would soon be promoted to supervisor over 5 restaurants. I had been GM for two progressively higher sales restaurants with the last one being the 5th highest sales in the chain and I had been the opening GM for a new concept that had strong growth.

An opportunity appeared that seemed good enough to at least take a close look. It had the additional benefit of being close to my then wife's parents since we had always lived far away.

The restaurant chain was medium size in number, around 20, I think, but at the time had the highest sales per unit in the United States. Not too shabby. The chain advertised that it was going to refresh the chain from top to bottom beginning with management, going away from hiring only relatives and relatives of relatives.

To this end, they hired a CEO from another modern restaurant chain and this CEO was beginning to hire experienced management from other chains to speed up modernization and expansion.

They were advertising that GM's would get a higher than competitive salary, benefits, company car, and 10% of the profits of the restaurant.

Hmmm. I would never get 10% of profits in my current chain and very, very few chains gave company cars. Mine sure didn't. Starting to sound very interesting.

They flew me up to talk to the CEO and visit a couple of the restaurants.

I loved the CEO; he was new and enthusiastic about revamping the chain, was passionate about hiring the very best managers he could, and was drawing up aggressive expansion plans.

He told me that I would be on the fast track and would be GM in 8 weeks.

OK. I'm in.

Sooooo, I turned in my resignation and became a trainee, then assistant manager, and sure enough, I was made GM in 8 weeks. All good so far. What could go wrong?

Well, the "car" turned out to be a station wagon. And not even a new station wagon. Definitely, not the BMW that I was expecting. Note to self: ASK what kind of car. Check.

Turns out the company "car" was expected to pick up liquor at the state liquor store for the restaurant, therefore the station wagon. Oh.

The GM was expected to only work the day shifts and the assistants only worked nights. While I personally loved this, I couldn't handle my assistants never seeing daylight, so I got permission to work one night shift per week.

But wait! There was the serious carrot of 10% profit of this very busy restaurant. That will more than make up for the company "car". Right?

In corporate restaurant chains, all managers can see the entire P&L from beginning to end.

Not here.

The GM could not see the back page. You know, the one with the profit on it.

So, let's see...10% times the profit...oh, wait, I can't see it.

Guess what? $10\% \times 0 = 0$

Yep. Nada. Zip. Nothing.

Kind of amazing that the restaurant never made a profit.

Then it got worse.

The CEO was fired.

I knew this was the beginning of the end for me because the owner was taking the company back to the family with relatives from top to bottom.

Sure enough, the environment changed drastically to stifling.

New ideas and "outsiders" were not welcome.

I was there one year exactly.

Lots and lots of lessons learned.

RESTAURANT CHAIN OR COUNTRY CLUB/ PRIVATE CLUB?

Private clubs include country, city, golf, equestrian, athletic, pool, yacht, tennis, and others. They are all private, meaning that there is some kind of membership required and the public cannot use the facilities. Like everything, there are pros and cons. Since private clubs have the same people coming in every day, managers get to know the members and the member families. In restaurants most guests are random. Restaurants do have regulars, of course, but think of private clubs as having only regulars.

There are two types of private clubs, equity and non-equity. In equity clubs, members actually own the club. The members pay an initial membership fee plus monthly dues. They have a board of directors who usually hire a professional club management company to actually run the day-to-day operations. The GM reports to the board of directors of the club, but also reports to the GM's boss at the management company. In non-equity clubs, the members don't own the club, but pay dues to a management company.

Pros of country club:

- Get to know members and their families
- Flat organization chart means good potential promotion
- Very good support through www.cmaa.org

Cons:

- No matter how well you're treated, you're not a member
- In a restaurant, if a guest is upset, they may not come back. In a private club, members are coming back. It's you who may not be coming back. Members, especially in equity clubs, are staying.
- In equity clubs, it can be difficult to report to the board and to your boss
- To find out more about country clubs and private clubs, visit the website of Club Management Association of America (www.cmaa.org)

RESTAURANT CHAIN OR MANAGED FOODSERVICE?

Managed foodservice is basically a foodservice company that works for a business whose business is not foodservice, like Microsoft or Ford Motor Company. This is a huge category, including hospital, university, military, sports stadiums, and corporate dining. Often, companies have both executive dining and employee dining.

Pros:

- Often closed on holidays and weekends
- Stable sales, since it is the company's employees that you are serving
- You're working when the company is working

Cons:

- Pretty much the same every day (con and pro)
- The largest players are probably Aramark and Sodexo.

OPENING YOUR OWN

Even if you have the money or could get the money, I would not recommend opening a restaurant without first being a general manager, having a great business plan, and great advisors. I know, because my first restaurant failed, and I thought I knew everything. After all, I was a very good manager, what could go wrong?

Well, pretty much everything can go wrong. Keep in mind that, as a manager, you are given the location, procedures, menu, kitchen equipment, layout, insurance, concept, policies, systems, leases, banking, and legal protections. But as an owner, you start with a blank page, with nothing given to you, yet you have to do it all. Yet most managers don't know squat about any of those. You can do it, but just know what you don't know.

BUYING AN EXISTING RESTAURANT THAT IS OPEN/CLOSED

This is easier than starting from scratch, but still difficult. Does the existing restaurant match the concept you had in mind? If you buy or start a restaurant that is not in your comfort zone (you love breakfast and lunch but you're looking at buying a full-service dinner and lunch restaurant), you will probably not do well. Research has shown that to make a closed restaurant into a new concept requires extensive remodeling, so your budget must include this. Does the equipment work with your menu? If it doesn't, you're spending money for nothing.

For a restaurant that is open, you must go over (and understand) the financial records that the current owner has given you with an accountant, including the Statement of Cash Flow and the Balance Sheet, not just the P & L. Can you trust the financials? Believe it or not, not all restaurant owners are totally honest. It is not all that difficult to exaggerate or downplay some of the figures on financial reports. One rough check for sales is to visit the restaurant on different days of the week and different meal periods. Count the number of customers in each period. Then multiply that by the check average for the meal period and then multiply it out for the month and add together. Do they roughly equal the sales shown on the P&L?

You are probably going to lease the building. Take the lease to a lawyer to go over it. Know before you sign.

OWNING BY YOURSELF OR WITH A PARTNER

The good news of owning it by yourself (sole proprietor) is that you get all the profit. The bad news is that you get all the losses. It's all yours. You also have the entire smarts of the restaurant. There is no one else to lean on unless you pay experts for their advice. With a partner, each of you have someone else to bounce ideas off and split the workload. Sole proprietor is also the easiest of the ownership possibilities to set up, basically just a tax number and you're off and running.

With a partnership, the main concern is to have a partnership agreement written BEFORE you do anything else. This document spells out each partner's responsibilities and what happens if the restaurant makes money, loses money, or if one of the partner's wants to bail out. The percentage of ownership usually, but not aways, depends upon the amount of money invested by each partner, though it could be that one partner receives a percentage of equity ownership for setting up, opening, and managing the restaurant instead of investing cash. Many really good friendships were destroyed because they didn't think they needed a partnership agreement.

CHAPTER 24

MY OWN SHIFTS FROM HELL

Everyone has had a shift from hell. Here are two of mine that I'll never forget.

#2

I was the general manager, and it was Memorial Day. I decided that I would work this holiday, giving my assistants a much deserved (and rare) holiday off.

I researched the sales for Memorial Day for the past two years and it showed that Memorial Day was really slow for both years. So, I staffed for slow and let off as many employees as I thought I could spare so they could enjoy the holiday. If I really needed extra help somewhere, a very good female manager in her last phase of training would be there, so I knew that she could help if needed.

I know you can tell where this is heading.

So, sure enough, it started out slow. Really slow. I was in the kitchen talking with my cooks when a server got my attention. He said the hostess was not seating him, but other servers were being seated.

I said OK, I'll be right there.

As I approached the hostess stand, I could see what looked like a couple hundred people standing around the young hostess, all trying to get her attention. When I got to the hostess, I could see that she was softly crying, and was basically paralyzed, not doing anything. She was trying to put people on a waiting list but crying as she just stood there, pen in hand. Then I looked beyond the hostess and there seemed to be another hundred people in the lobby crowding around.

Being the very sharp, quick, and experienced manager that I was, I thought: This is not good.

But no problem. I'll get my manager trainee.

Not so fast, grasshopper. That was when it went from not good to very bad. Very bad.

The bar was packed, every seat at every table filled. I looked at the manager trainee as she was taking an order. She too was crying as she bravely took drink orders.

I know I had to do something. But, what? That was the question.

With nothing to lose, I gathered up the first four groups in the lobby and sat them in the first four tables. I continued to do this until the lobby was clear. Then I started in the bar until all my servers were maxed out. I figured the servers could be trusted to bust their butts and do at least a pretty good job.

I then ran into the kitchen alerting the cooks that they were about to get slammed. My hostess recovered enough to help as did the manager trainee. Together we helped the servers as much as possible. After the servers went through their turn of chaos, I moved to the kitchen to help as much as possible as they went through their chaos.

All in all, a really, really suck evening. I was physically and emotionally wiped out. I thought about saving all the customers some time by giving each customer my name and the name of my supervisor so they would know who to complain to.

I thought about it but didn't.

• • • •

#1

Have you ever had one of those days when everything went wrong and all yo   u wanted to do was go home, grab a beer, turn on the TV, watch anything, and just unwind?

Here we go.

The story begins on a Friday night…the restaurant was busy as hell, lines out the door, but it was going ok. No serious problems, except that we were a little shorthanded, so I had to buzz around quite a bit. I was really looking forward for the night to end. It was about a half hour before closing when I got a frantic tugging at my arm that the toilets had overflowed.

No problem. No big deal. I grabbed a busser, sent him in to clean it up, and forgot about it.

Then I got a report from the kitchen that the kitchen drains were all backing up and it was really getting wet in there. I go into the kitchen and sure enough, the floor was wet with water coming in through the drain lines. Lots of it. Fast. Did I say lots? Time for the plumber. I needed professional help now.

The water continued to rise. It didn't take long for the kitchen to be under 1 inch of water, then 2 inches. By now the water was starting to leak out into the dining room. Did I mention that this wasn't just water, but sewage water? Oh, yeah. And you can imagine that the water did not smell exactly great either.

I was in the kitchen with a mop when a hostess comes in to say that she was starting to get lots of complaints about the smell. Would I do something, please? The kitchen was totally flooded now with everyone just about ankle deep. The only one who was enjoying himself was the dishwasher, who loved that everyone was smelling and looking like he usually smelled and looked.

I turned around to talk to the hostess, when I slipped. Right into the muck. I fell totally flat. About a 9.3 in the new Olympic event of manager-slipping-in sewage-in-kitchen. I was sopping wet, not feeling real good. I was wet, frustrated, and smelly.

I couldn't leave to change since I was the only manager. I put on a cook's shirt from the office, which was too small because we had just given out all the larger ones. But, it was clean, which meant it was fine, even though it was really tight and looked ridiculous on me.

The plumber arrived late of course. By the time the plumber had finished, and I had mopped the kitchen by myself, (I had sent everyone home because it was so late), I was totally beat. It was around 3:30 AM in the morning. I finally got in my car to head home.

Little did I know that this night was just starting.

I was driving home when I spotted two guys next to a car who were trying to get someone to stop to help them.

I stopped.

What the hell; misery loves company. They said they had run out of gas and asked if I could give them a ride to a gas station? Sure, hop in. I drove to an all-night gas station. While I waited in the car, they went in to get some gas and coffee. As we drove back to their car with the gas, a police car gets in back of me, turns on its lights, and starts the siren right behind me.

I stopped.

He pulls out his gun and yells: "Get out and spread 'em!" It turns out that while my boys were in the gas station, they were also robbing the place. The gas station guy called the police and here we are!

It took a while before I convinced the policeman that I was not part of this entire deal, that I had just tried to help the hitchhikers. The policeman said he had heard that one before, but the guys helped me and actually said the same thing. I then showed the policeman where I had picked them up by their (stolen) car.

I was finally allowed to go home. As I pulled into the garage, the paper was being delivered, the sun was coming up, and now a beer sounded much better than coffee.

THANKS FOR READING!

If this book has been of value to you,
I would greatly appreciate if you would leave a review.

Made in the USA
Coppell, TX
28 October 2022